THE POWER OF ZERO:
LEARNING FROM THE WORLD'S LEADING NET ZERO ENERGY BUILDINGS

An Ecotone Publishing Book/2016
Copyright © 2016 International Living Future Institute

Ecotone Publishing – an Imprint of International Living Future Institute

For more information write:

Ecotone Publishing
721 NW Ninth Avenue, Suite 195
Portland, OR 97209

Author: Brad Liljequist
Book Design: softfirm
Editor: Fred McLennan
Consulting Editor: Jess Chamberlain

Library of Congress Control Number: 2015955099

Library of Congress Cataloging-in Publication Data
ISBN: 978-0-9827749-5-3

1. ARCHITECTURE   2. ENGINEERING   3. ENVIRONMENT

First Edition

Printed in Altona, Manitoba, Canada
on FSC-certified paper, Processed Chlorine-Free, using vegetable-based ink.

TABLE OF CONTENTS

05   Introduction
by Amanda Sturgeon

PART I:
THE NET ZERO CONCEPT

10   What is Net Zero
Energy?

15   The Net Zero Revolution:
Addressing Our
Generation's Challenge

23   Extraction, Refining,
and Transportation
Impacts on People and
Nature – The Equity
Connection

PART II:
NET ZERO PROJECTS

30   The Search for
Efficiency

34   Getting to
Net Zero Energy –
Design Process

RESIDENTIAL BUILDINGS

38   zHome
ISSAQUAH, WA

50   Willowbrook
House
AUSTIN, TX

56   Zero Energy House
AUCKLAND, NZ

62   Mission Zero House
ANN ARBOR, MI

68   Zero Cottage
SAN FRANCISCO, CA

COMMERCIAL AND
OFFICE BUILDINGS

78   David & Lucile
Packard Foundation
Headquarters
LOS ALTOS, CA

88   DPR Construction
Phoenix Regional
Headquarters
PHOENIX, AZ

96   IDeAs Z^2 Design Facility
SAN JOSE, CA

102   Bullitt Center
SEATTLE, WA

116   American Samoa
EPA Office
**UTULEI,
AMERICAN SAMOA**

INSTITUTIONAL BUILDINGS

124   Tyson Living
Learning Center
EUREKA, MO

130   Smith College's
Bechtel Environmental
Classroom
WHATLEY, MA

136   Hawaii Preparatory
Academy Energy Lab
KAMUELA, HI

146   Hood River Middle
School Music and
Science Building
HOOD RIVER, OR

152 Sacred Heart Lower
and Middle School
Stevens Library
ATHERTON, CA

160 West Berkeley
Public Library
BERKELEY, CA

168 Omega Center for
Sustainable Living
RHINEBECK, NY

174 Center for Sustainable
Landscapes at Phipps
Conservatory and
Botanical Gardens
PITTSBURGH, PA

184 Painters Hall
SALEM, OR

189 EUI Comparison

190 Net Zero Energy
Challenge

PART III:
NET ZERO COMMUNITIES

195 Complexity and the
Human Factor

197 Issues Around
Net Zero Communities

203 Legacy Case Studies

**HOCKERTON
HOUSING PROJECT**

**THE VAUBAN
NEIGHBORHOOD**

206 Planning for Net Zero
Energy Communities

**NOE VALLEY,
SAN FRANCISCO, CA**

SOUTH UPTON, NORMAL, IL

DISTRICT OF COLUMBIA

PART IV:
A NET POSITIVE FUTURE

217 Net Zero Energy
Building Design
and Technologies –
The Next Generation

219 The End Game

225 Conclusion

APPENDIX

226 Acknowledgements

228 Domain of Knowledge

230 Glossary

232 About ILFI + Credits

West Berkeley Public Library, Berkeley, CA

4

WHAT DOES GOOD LOOK LIKE?

That is a question that we ask everyday through the Living Building Challenge program. The global movement towards Living Buildings is growing as the realization sets in that global climate change is real and solutions such as net zero energy are possible.

"Good" looks like a building that generates enough energy for its own needs, operates pollution free and provides inspiration for people to make change in their everyday lives. The pathway towards good buildings and communities is not easy because the viable options are not yet clearly defined and the journey to discover solutions is fraught with challenges that take persistence and determination to reveal. With rapidly increasing global temperatures and record-setting droughts we, as a society, can no longer make incremental, isolated, and reactive remedies; we must take wide-scale transformative action.

The majority of energy generated today comes from highly polluting and often politically destabilizing sources such as coal, gas, oil and nuclear power. The effects of these energy sources on regional and planetary health are becoming increasingly evident through climate change, the most worrisome major global trend attributed to human activity.

It is time to envision a safe, reliable and decentralized power grid, powered entirely by renewable energy, supplied to incredibly efficient buildings and infrastructure without the negative externalities associated with combustion. Net zero energy buildings and communities will make this vision possible.

A net zero energy building is a demonstration of what is possible when we visualize a Living Future that is ecologically restorative, socially just, and culturally rich. A net zero energy building feels different; the occupants use lights only when needed and they control their own indoor climate through adjustments to windows and shades, enhancing their connection to, and understanding of, the outside environment. These daily and seasonal patterns of behavior are not so different from those of our ancestors

"These Net Zero Energy Buildings are beacons of hope that provide a platform to inform other efforts throughout the world and accelerate the implementation of restorative principles. *The Power of Zero* brings these beacons of hope alive and explores the steps that each project took to reduce its energy demand and, in several cases, become the most efficient buildings in North America. As the newly released Living Community Challenge gets traction it is taking the concept of Net Zero Energy to the community and city scale."

who relied on natural lighting, heating, and cooling strategies.

However, with the introduction of mechanical heating and air conditioning, many parts of the world diverted from this working with nature approach. We are now passive occupants in our buildings instead of active participants. We have come to accept the lack of natural light, disconnection from the outside environment, and the stale air that is delivered through air conditioning systems. Society has separated from nature and we no longer expect that our buildings will connect us to it.

In the United States, passive solar design had resurgence during the oil crisis of the 1970s; the U.S. Department of Energy was created in 1977 and much pioneering work was done to explore what a net zero energy building might look like. As the oil situation improved and the political climate changed this work became dwarfed by business as usual. While green building became prevalent in the 1990s it was not until the early 2000s that the concept of net zero energy buildings reemerged, in part as a response to the impact that building energy use has on global climate change. We are at a pivotal time in the net zero energy movement; a combination of political and ethical will in the United States is driving the economics and technology to make net zero energy not only possible but also mainstream. It is a moment in time that has been forty years in the making.

As more net zero energy buildings emerged over the last decade, the International Living Future Institute identified that a Net Zero Energy Building Certification would legitimize the claim of reaching a net zero target. Performance based, there are now twenty-one Net Zero Energy certified projects; most of them are featured in this book. Certification allows us to explore in detail the lessons learned and the success stories for performance knowing that there is a common benchmark and performance period across all projects.

For the projects featured within *The Power of Zero*, the concept of living within the carrying capacity of the place and using natural resources such as the sun and wind to their maximum potential begins when the building is first conceived. To start a building design process by determining the size and type of building through the amount of energy that can be generated on the site causes the design and development team to work collaboratively and to approach the building as if people and nature are interconnected.

These Net Zero Energy Buildings are beacons of hope that provide a platform to inform other efforts throughout the world and accelerate the implementation of restorative principles. *The Power of Zero* brings these beacons of hope alive and explores the steps that each project took to reduce its energy demand and, in several cases, become the most efficient buildings in North America. As the newly released Living Community Challenge gets traction it is taking the concept of Net Zero Energy to the community and city scale.

The Bullitt Center in Seattle, for example, has shown the world that it is not only possible for a six-story urban office building to generate enough energy for its own use from solar panels on its roof, but that it is also possible to be net positive and produce surplus energy due to exemplary energy conservation strategies such as highly efficient wall and window systems. The building uses simple technology to achieve an incredible 85 percent reduction in energy, all the while increasing the comfort of its occupants compared to a regular office building.

Net zero energy is quickly becoming a sought-after goal for many buildings around the globe and while these net zero energy buildings are still few in number, the ILFI predicts their time has come. Each of the projects in this book is the result of an intense commitment by the building owner, the design and construction team, as well as the occupants. Together they are defining "What Good Looks Like" and helping us move towards a Living Future that will allow all life to thrive.

AMANDA STURGEON, FAIA

PART I

THE NET ZERO CONCEPT

WHAT IS NET ZERO ENERGY?

The International Living Future Institute defines Net Zero Energy (NZE) as "One hundred percent of the project's energy needs being supplied by on-site renewable energy on a net annual basis." In one simple, elegant sentence, a radical agenda for eliminating carbon dioxide emissions and use of combustion fuels within the built environment is set in place. In short: generate what you use. With this crisp idea, an array of powerful forces and concepts are brought to bear on some of our time's most challenging problems.

Restated in more basic terms, Net Zero Energy buildings and communities generate as much energy as they use over the course of the year. The significant majority of NZE buildings are connected to the grid, with a meter that spins backwards and forwards: when the building is generating more than it uses it builds a surplus, and when it uses more than it generates, it draws from that surplus. At the end of the year, at a minimum it nets to zero use, or potentially is net positive. In practice, NZE buildings have to significantly lower the energy use from typical consumption — usually a 60-80 percent reduction. On-site energy generation offsets the remaining use.

Net zero energy is such a radical and powerful concept because it is one of the key solutions to carbon neutrality and the elimination of fossil fuel use. If we apply favorite Institute questions of "What is the end game?," and, "What if everyone did it?" to net zero energy, the end result would be massively positive. By sector, energy use in buildings is the largest single contributor to our carbon footprint — roughly 40 percent, depending on the estimate. If all current buildings were retrofitted to be net zero energy, and all new construction was built to a net zero standard, society's collective carbon footprint would be reduced by that amount.

The Power of Zero is dedicated to practical, real examples of these buildings in a range of types, sizes, and places which achieve net zero energy usage. The existence of these projects means that net zero energy is a real, viable solution to what is likely the most significant threat to global stability currently in existence, on par with the threat of nuclear proliferation. Remaking our communities to be net zero energy

UNITED STATES ENERGY USE BY SECTOR

30%
INDUSTRY

29%
TRANSPORTATION

41%
BUILDING

RESIDENTIAL 22%
COMMERCIAL 19%

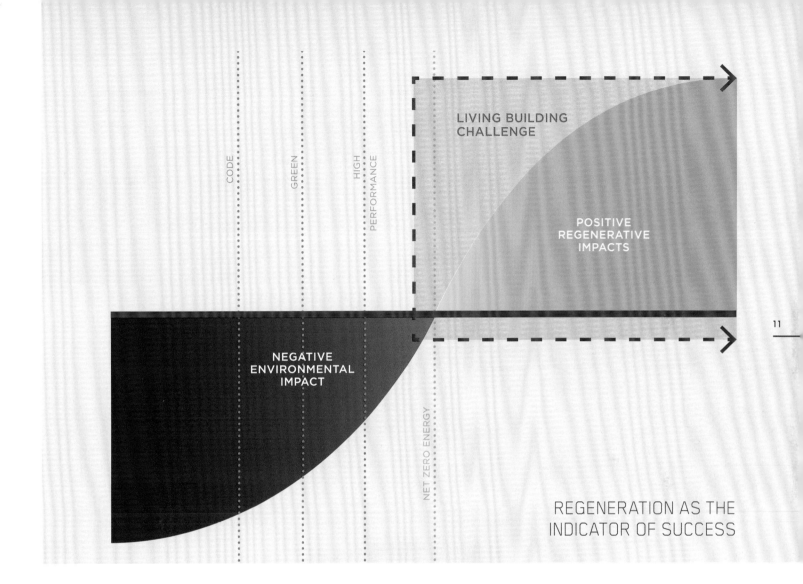

CODE

GREEN

HIGH PERFORMANCE

LIVING BUILDING CHALLENGE

POSITIVE REGENERATIVE IMPACTS

NEGATIVE ENVIRONMENTAL IMPACT

NET ZERO ENERGY

REGENERATION AS THE INDICATOR OF SUCCESS

11

is more than a neat exercise in efficiency. It is a moral imperative to protect those people most impacted by climate change and ocean acidification — those in the developing world and future generations. It eliminates one of the major drivers of military action (acquisition and protection of energy supplies) and degradation of local wilderness in the form of extraction impacts.

Within the framework of the International Living Future Institute's thinking about human development and living in restorative harmony with the Earth, net zero energy stands as a gateway. Energy in all its forms is a key component of life; living in a way that draws vitality from within, instead of exchanging resources from others without positive return, is the way of nature. To our peril much of

historic Western development has ignored this pattern of synergistic exchange, now to our peril. Net zero energy is the first opening into a new way of approaching what we make and dwell in, asking the question: How do our actions add to rather than subtract from energy supplies? Net positive energy, at its heart, is a biomimetic reflection of energy flows within nature.

In less philosophical but more practical, metaphoric terms, net zero energy represents old time, traditional values.

Living within your means

One of the most conservative values is to live in a way that does not exceed what you have. You do not eat your seed corn, and you take responsibility for yourself and family.

Thou shalt not steal

The unfortunate reality is that many of our resources have been obtained through power relationships that exceed a just exchange between the recipients and givers. Perhaps most compellingly, it is clear at this point that we are taking our descendants' heritage from them, as they will bear the brunt of our irresponsibility in energy use and its impacts.

A penny saved is a penny earned

Our grandparents' generation knew the value of simply using less. Net zero energy buildings and communities squeeze out every watt of savings possible. These buildings are not just resilient in their interaction with the Earth, but also in their long term basic demands of operating costs, providing an essentially conservative financial platform of living.

Reap the harvest

A foundational concept of human civilization is that we organize and systematize the gathering of the fruits of the Earth. For millennia that idea has primarily referred to a harvest of food. With new technologies and paradigms, it also can mean harvesting the energy provided by the Earth — the sun, wind (really solar energy), and tides.

Mottainai

Derived from an old Shinto concept that material objects have souls, this Japanese word embodies meanings of both wastefulness and irreverence. More recently, Kenyan Nobel Peace Prize winner Wangari Matthai sought to popularize the term internationally as a way to place a sense of the sacred on our thoughtful use of resources.

Net zero energy is also a very compelling concept to the general public, which crystalizes core needs of dramatic energy reduction and renewable energy generation into one simple, easy-to-understand idea. While it can be very challenging to excite the average person about the sometimes arcane world of energy efficiency, net zero energy has a demonstrated ability to inspire and involve people. NZE brings forward a can-do spirit which combines the best of applied technology and design, Buck Rogers, and big jumps forward. It is also an accessible, inspiring response to people beleaguered by a sense of hopelessness around larger energy use and climate problems.

Net zero energy buildings represent the beginning of a new era of innovation within the world of buildings. Amazingly, homes in much of the world are still built the way they were one hundred years ago. Within North America, balloon framing pioneered in the 1800s is still the standard. It is as if we still drove Ford Model T's instead of electric vehicles, or used mechanical adding machines instead of computers. In most other sectors, the performance characteristics of the desired object tend to drive technological development, while in the building sector, the technologies have tended to define the design. We hopefully stand at the beginning of a new era of building design evolution, which reflects a whole array of human and environmental needs, only one of which includes eliminating the energy footprint of the built environment.

A key component of innovation to achieve net zero energy performance is a deep drive towards designing with nature, the laws of physics, and biomimetics. Net zero energy buildings take advantage of diurnal temperature swings, and available naturally stored thermal energy, capturing and retaining what is needed to serve the building. The gift of the sun, from which all life springs, is fully embraced, through daylight, heat, wind, and photons. Many of the key technologies used in net zero energy buildings respond to natural phenomena,

Rooftop of Zero Cottage in San Francisco

13

such as evaporative cooling, stack effect, the ideal gas law, and gas/liquid/solid phase changes. Some of these phenomena are described in more detail in section three, below.

As part of its net zero and net positive energy requirements, the Institute prohibits the use of on-site combustion. There are a number of reasons for this prohibition. Typically, building related combustion involves so-called "natural" gas, which adds CO_2 to the atmosphere and oceans. Eliminating its use is a major priority of the ILFI. Extensive use of woody biomass removes critical material from natural cycles, and in many cases accelerates climate change by speeding up the slower release of CO_2 through decay. Biogas supplies can prove transitory, and easily default to natural gas. Depending on the type of combustion, local air quality impacts can be significant. While it is recognized that most net zero energy buildings are connected to a grid which is reliant on the larger energy grid, of which natural gas and coal burning power plants currently play a significant role, the Institute's

ZHOME

When was the last time 10,000 people spent an hour or two touring a townhome community?

zHome, in Issaquah, WA, was conceptualized as a project to give hope in a time of despair about what to do about climate change. This ten-home community was led by a small city in suburban Seattle, and supported by an array of community partners, including the regional government and local utility.

When the project was completed, a major education/inspiration program was held over nine weekends, teaching area residents about high performance envelopes, heat pumps, and solar panels. Supported by an extensive regional media campaign, hundreds received in-depth tours each day; in many cases participants came from hundreds of miles away. A noticeable aspect of the attendees was that they came from a wide array of backgrounds and interests.

zHome shows a deep hunger for climate solutions within average people.

end goal is a fully renewable energy grid which includes the complete elimination of combustion, particularly of fossil fuels. Impacts of combustion are discussed further in the section below, and the end state vision of the grid is discussed in Part IV.

Finally, in 2013, the Institute launched the Net Positive conference in San Francisco, California, indicating a conceptual shift in net zero energy. Version 3.0 of the Living Building Challenge evolved the Energy Petal to require 105 percent of a building's energy use to be offset by on-site

generation, rather than 100 percent. At the same time, the Institute has strengthened and extended its Net Zero Energy Building certification. In terms of actual change in energy generation, the amounts are relatively modest. In concept, however, the evolution of net zero to net positive is significant: nature does not do zero. Natural systems tend to be fecund and generous, providing a bounty beyond what the individual needs. Net positive energy is a libation of abundance, a ray of goodwill and intention to our neighbors and the future.

THE NET ZERO REVOLUTION: ADDRESSING OUR GENERATION'S CHALLENGE

Perhaps the benefits of net zero energy buildings are self evident, but the bottom line truth is that the voracity of our current energy use threatens to unhinge the platform of tenuous security our global civilization rests on. Our energy use certainly threatens the planet and biodiversity, but also threatens ourselves. In aggregate, these impacts add up to a significant potential destabilization and, in the case of ocean acidification, has a more significant possibility of interrupting the deeper chain of life which springs from our oceans.

Each era has had major threats to civilization stability, including:
• Epidemics
• Foreign invasion
• Religious wars
• Resource wars
• Genocide
• Drought
• Nuclear war and winter

Some of these threats were well understood at the time, and the societies responded as well as they could. At other times the threats were not recognized, nor understood.

The previous generation confronted perhaps the most existential threat humanity has known — the threat of nuclear war and winter (of course,

this threat continues, though the risk is diminished). This threat was highly challenging, and the path to resolve it was very unclear. The possibility of failure was potentially devastating. Regardless of one's beliefs about the outcome, clearly there was a response. Between 1940 and 1996, the United States alone spent $5.5 trillion on its nuclear arsenal. Much of the residual of that effort continues to today. By comparison, the United States only invested $311 billion in clean energy between 2004 and 2013. The order of magnitude of our response must jump a level to match our last generation's effort.

At the time of the publication of this book, we find ourselves in a strange place emotionally relative to our energy use. On one hand, large portions of the American population have adopted a know-nothing, antiscientific approach to climate change, and the significant majority of the global political establishment refuses to lead a path out of negative patterns of energy use. Furthermore, there continues to be a gap of understanding of the plethora of solutions and alternative pathways to much more benign and even positive energy usage. On the other hand, there are, in fact, energy solutions — many of them — which are quickly becoming economical and available.

The rapid technological advancement and price reduction of LED lighting, electric vehicles, and photovoltaic panels are a few key examples. One could be forgiven for feeling they are witnessing theatre, wondering whether the forces of good or ill will win out. So where do we stand with regard to the problems associated with our current patterns of energy usage?

Climate Change

If you are reading this book, it is likely that you are quite familiar with climate change, and are working to limit its impact. In fact, it may be the main reason you are interested in net zero energy buildings. However, the science continues to expand and be refined, and the latest data and forecasts are becoming ever more alarming. In 2014, the Intergovernmental Panel on Climate Change (IPCC) released its fifth report, the 2014 Climate Change Synthesis Report. The Synthesis Report found the following (quoted verbatim to provide accuracy):

• The period from 1983 to 2012 was likely the warmest 30-year period of the last 1400 years in the Northern Hemisphere, where such assessment is possible (medium confidence).

• Ocean warming dominates the increase in energy stored in the climate system, accounting for more than 90 percent of the energy accumulated between 1971 and 2010 (high confidence).

- Since the beginning of the industrial era, oceanic uptake of CO_2 has resulted in acidification of the ocean; the pH of ocean surface water has decreased by 0.1 (high confidence), corresponding to a 26 percent increase in acidity.

- Extreme precipitation events over most of the mid-latitude land masses and over wet tropical regions will very likely become more intense and more frequent.

- A large fraction of species faces increased extinction risk due to climate change during and beyond the 21st century, especially as climate change interacts with other stressors (high confidence). Most plant species cannot naturally shift their geographical ranges sufficiently fast to keep up with current and high projected rates of climate change in most landscapes; most small mammals and freshwater molluscs will not be able to keep up at the rates projected under RCP4.5 and above in flat landscapes in this century (high confidence).

- Global temperature increases of ~4°C or more above late 20th century levels, combined with increasing food demand, would pose large risks to food security globally (high confidence).

- Climate change is projected to reduce renewable surface water and groundwater resources in most

"Iceberg with hole" by Brocken Inaglory - Own work. Licensed under CC BY-SA 3.0 via Wikimedia Commons.

dry subtropical regions (robust evidence, high agreement),

- Throughout the 21st century, climate change is expected to lead to increases in ill-health in many regions and especially in developing countries with low income, as compared to a baseline without climate change (high confidence).

- By 2100 for RCP8.5 [the most extreme projection], the combination of high temperature and humidity in some areas for parts of the year is expected to compromise common human activities, including growing food and working outdoors (high confidence).

- Surface temperatures will remain approximately constant at elevated levels for many centuries after a complete cessation of net anthropogenic CO_2 emissions. A large fraction of anthropogenic climate change resulting from CO_2 emissions is irreversible on a multi-century to millennial timescale.

Some have said the IPCC reporting is overly alarmist, but in fact the opposite is true — because it is subject to such heavy scrutiny, the IPCC tends to be very cautious in its statements.

THE PRECAUTIONARY PRINCIPLE

The ILFI frames its thinking around a number of core principles. The Precautionary Principle is one of the most significant of these tenets. Simply put, it means erring on the side of caution in the face of the unknown, and considering the potential impacts and ramifications of an action. When potential downside risks are substantial, the path of prudence is taken. It is a fundamentally conservative principle, since it prioritizes stability and continuity over the potentially negative. The Precautionary Principle illuminates much of the Institute's approach to materials and The Red List – where any evidence indicates potential health impacts of a material, it is avoided. Applying the Precautionary Principle to climate change, even though there is not 100 percent certainty about the exact outcome, enough concern has been raised that we should fully respond. In fact, the Precautionary Principle would dictate that with even more ambiguous scientific consensus, we should still fully respond, given the massive impacts that are being highlighted by the science.

17

OCEAN ACIDIFICATION –
Climate Change's Lesser Known, Evil Twin

If the specifics of the rate of change, on the ground impact, and timing of climate change are unclear, the simplicity of the science about ocean acidification is such that it leaves no room for doubt, and demands immediate action. This phenomena has arisen abruptly and disconcertingly, giving credence to the Precautionary Principle and unforeseen impacts. Significant impacts are being felt now.

The science of ocean acidification starts simply, but then becomes somewhat more complicated chemically as ocean mixing occurs. As CO_2 in the atmosphere increases, about 28 percent of it is absorbed by the oceans. The CO_2 in the ocean then combines with H_2O to form carbonic acid, H_2CO_3. Carbonic acid is the same chemical that gives the fizz to soda pop. The carbonic acid then goes through a more complicated range of chemical reactions, resulting in a reduction in two key ingredients needed for growing shells: aragonite and calcite. Alarmingly, the acidity of the oceans has risen by 30 percent since the beginning of the industrial age. The results are already being deeply felt in an array of places — three of which are highlighted below.

> "To put the possible environmental changes facing us into some perspective, one would have to turn the clock back at least 100 million years to find analogous surface ocean pH conditions."
>
> RIDGWELL AND ZEEBE (2005)

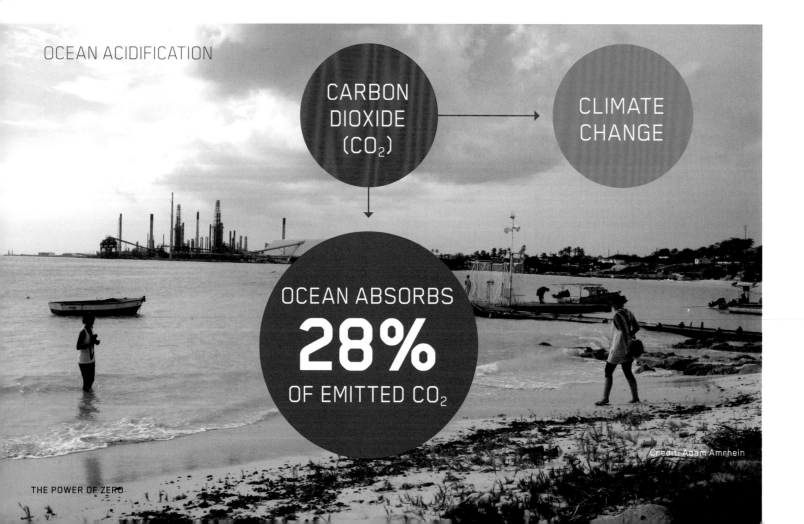

OCEAN ACIDIFICATION

CARBON DIOXIDE (CO_2)

CLIMATE CHANGE

OCEAN ABSORBS 28% OF EMITTED CO_2

Credit: Adam Amrhein

THE POWER OF ZERO

Coral reefs

Ocean reefs are considered to be the places of the greatest biodiversity anywhere on Earth, with between 600,000 and nine million reef species supported by the habitat they provide. These massive colonial calciferous organisms, slowly building on past selves, are also impacted by ocean acidification.

Different types of reefs rely on either calcite or aragonite to form, and reduced saturation of these building blocks in the ocean impacts their ability to grow. The death of coral reefs, serious enough as it is, has the much larger ramification of then removing habitat for the vast array of life that relies on it to live. Even though reefs cover less than 1 percent of the ocean floor, they harbor about 25 percent of all ocean life. Since most of these reefs are in coastal, warmer waters, their demise is particularly of concern to poorer, less developed countries where coastal fisheries are a critical element of the food supply. The long term concern over the death of the reefs is a crash of biodiversity in the oceans, with widespread impacts on the chain of life overall.

"Before the industrial revolution, more than 98 percent of corals reefs were surrounded by waters that were →3.5 times saturated with respect to their skeleton materials (aragonite). If atmospheric CO_2 is stabilized at 450 ppm, only 8 percent of existing coral reefs will be surrounded by water with this saturation level."

CAO AND CALDERIA (2008)

Willapa Bay OysterBed
Photo by TaraSchmidt,
Flickr CC

Washington Coast Oyster Farms

Beginning in 2005, seed oysters grown in Willapa Bay, on the Washington State Pacific coast, began dying literally by the billions. Science around ocean acidification, incredibly still in its infancy, began to suggest it as the source of the die off. Willapa Bay oyster harvesting, done for millennia by the Lower Chehalis and Willapa Chinook tribes, and commercialized by Europeans in the late 1800s with non-native oysters, began to come to an end in one of the first major on-the-ground impact of CO_2 emissions. The $100 million a year Washington oyster industry is now at risk; upwelling of acidic water along the Pacific coast is resulting in lower levels of calcite in the water, so baby oysters no longer can grow. Because oysters in Willapa Bay no longer regenerate naturally, some oyster farmers now must obtain their seed oysters in other areas. One oyster farm, Goose Point Oyster Company on the Long Beach peninsula, has opened a $1 million oyster seed growing facility on Hawai'i and flies its seed oyster to then be planted in Willapa Bay. This interruption of the natural chain of life only occurred within the last decade. And the evolution of the basic science since then indicates that many unknowns, some potentially very significant, exist in our future.

Pteropods

Perhaps the most disconcerting current impact of ocean acidification is the loss of pteropods, due to their inability to form their micron thick shells. These tiny crustaceans, which are about 1/8 to ½ inch in size, are nicknamed the "sea butterfly", and are a critical ocean food source.

In a recent U.S. National Oceanographic and Atmospheric Adminstration/Oregon State University study along the northern Pacific coast of the United States, 53 percent of the pteropods sampled had severely dissolved shells. This achingly painful fact took all involved offguard. It highlights the nature of how the CO_2 uptake process actually interfaces with ocean current, temperature, and flow dynamics. Acidified, calcite and aragonite depleted water tends to stratify and concentrate in the ocean, and at certain times is moving onto coastal areas, where it has significant impacts on crusteceans such as the pteropod.

"We did not expect to see pteropods being affected to this extent in our coastal region for several decades."

WILLIAM PETERSON, Ph.D., OCEANOGRAPHER, NOAA NORTHWEST FISHERIES SCIENCE CENTER, 2014

A pteropod die off could have critical impacts on the ocean chain of life. In certain years, pteropods make up more than 50 percent of the diet of juvenile Pink salmon, but they are also eaten by anchovies, herring, mackerel, sablefish, and Coho, Chum, and Sockeye salmon, as well as zooplankton, squid, whales, and birds. Many of these become food for larger fish farther up the food chain, such as tuna, salmon, and pollock, creating second order impacts. While the story of Willapa Bay oysters focuses on a non-native species, which potentially evolved in areas with different ocean chemistry, the pteropod put the spotlight squarely on what is potentially one of the very first real, on-the-ground impacts of our CO_2 emissions.

All three of these stories highlight uncertainty and the unknown. In 2005, after decades of discussion about climate change, we were surprised to see our earlier predictions upended. Once again, application of the Precautionary Principle is called for — would we really consider any of these impacts to be acceptable on a Living Planet?

21

Pteropod, nicknamed the sea butterfly, swimming in seawater with low surface CO_2 conditions that preserve the shell with no dissolution.

"Iraq possesses huge reserves of oil and gas – reserves I'd love Chevron to have access to..."

KENNETH DERR,
CEO OF CHEVRON,
SPEAKING TO THE
COMMONWEALTH
CLUB OF SAN
FRANCISCO IN 1998

U.S. Army Sgt. Mark Phiffer stands guard duty near a burning oil well in the Rumaylah Oil Fields in Southern Iraq. U.S. Navy photo by Photographer's Mate 1st Class Arlo K. Abrahamson. Wikimedia Commons

Securing Energy Supplies

Between 1976 and 2007, the United States spent $7.3 trillion defending the Persian Gulf alone. This is equal to nearly half of the US GDP in 2013. Incredibly, it amounts to $59,000 per U.S. household, enough to convert every home in the United States to net zero energy usage, and then some. A 2013 study found that the U.S. invasion of Iraq led to the death of about one half million Iraqis. While Iraq's prior leadership was responsible for the death of many thousands, the simple fact is that the need to defend access to and stability of global energy supplies resulted in the death of more Iraqis than Americans were killed in World War II, in a much smaller country. The first U.S.-Iraq conflict, the Gulf War, also led to the greatest oil spill in history, deliberately caused by retreating Iraqi troops in 1991. The size of this spill was twice the size of the Deepwater Horizon spill, discussed below. The Persian

"Of course it's about oil; we can't really deny that..."

GEN. JOHN ABIZAID,
THEN HEAD OF U.S.
CENTRAL COMMAND
AND MILITARY
OPERATIONS IN IRAQ,
IN 2007, SPEAKING
ABOUT THE IRAQ WAR

"Oil remains fundamentally a government business. While many regions of the world offer great oil opportunities, the Middle East with two thirds of the world's oil and the lowest cost, is still where the prize ultimately lies, even though companies are anxious for greater access there, progress continues to be slow."

FORMER US SECRETARY OF DEFENSE AND VICE PRESIDENT
DICK CHENEY, AT A SPEECH DELIVERED AT THE LONDON
INSTITUTE OF PETROLEUM, 1999

Gulf has yet to recover fully from this disaster, particularly in coastal salt marshes, critical habitat for biodiversity.

This is simply one example. Other energy source hot spots abound. Today, China is building artificial islands in the South China Sea, to extend its territorial claims to cover oil rich marine areas. Indonesia is responding by building a nearby military base. In another, very significant example, about 30 percent of Europe's natural gas supply comes from Russia, an increasingly volatile player which shut off natural gas deliveries to the Ukraine in 2014. The dependence by Europe on this energy gives Russia additional leverage in its potential aggression on its neighbors.

EXTRACTION, REFINING, AND TRANSPORTATION IMPACTS ON PEOPLE AND NATURE – THE EQUITY CONNECTION

The campaign for energy independence has had negative consequences, however. As nations seek to supply their energy internally, they are forced to confront the real impacts of energy extraction, refinement, and creation.

Oil Extraction

Removing oil from the ground significantly degrades the wild and local human communities. From the Arctic to the Niger Delta, from the boreal forests of Canada to the Amazon jungle of Venezuela, oil extraction has a negative impact on local people and nature. Like many

of the other impacts of petroleum use, extraction bears heavily on less advantaged communities.

One specific example is the Oginiland portion of the Niger River Delta of Nigeria. The United Nations Environmental Program recently performed an in-depth study of the area, looking at the long-term impacts of decades of oil extraction. This area, home to 850,000 people and an array of wildlife, has been extensively impacted by oil. Impacts include:

- Extensive deep soil contamination

- Groundwater contamination at 41 sites

- All streams and wetlands significantly degraded and covered in hydrocarbons and tar

- Heavy reduction in fish and fisheries

- Air benzene levels exceeding USEPA and WHO levels

Refining

Even within the developed world, where oil refining frequently occurs, petrochemical impacts are often significant, and frequently have the most effect on disadvantaged communities. For example, within Louisiana, 200,000 people live within two miles of refineries. In Manchester, Texas, home of a major Valero refinery, children are 56 percent more likely to have leukemia than those from ten miles away. A 2010 EPA study revealed that eight known health impacting chemicals exceeded acceptable levels in air quality sampling. Now, incredibly, the Keystone XL pipeline is proposed to be routed through the community, and much of its oil refined in area refineries.

Spills

Despite its assertions to the contrary, the oil industry simply cannot avoid major periodic spills which have devastating environmental consequences. The industry is moving its way north, into the Arctic, now made available by the sea ice melting caused by the very same actor. This now brings the spill threat to yet another new, fragile, untrammeled ecosystem.

Fire boat response crews battle the blazing remnants of the off shore oil rig Deepwater Horizon April 21, 2010. Photo: U.S. Coast Guard

23

The Deepwater Horizon explosion and spill, which occurred in 2010, is a case study on the potential consequences of petrochemical extraction. This disaster resulted in eleven deaths and five million barrels of oil being released directly into the environment. Five years later, its impacts continue to weigh heavily on the Gulf of Mexico. Tellingly, only 25 percent of the released oil can even be accounted for. Ongoing impacts include tar layers in coastal wetlands, oil vapors, and consolidated weathered oil within the water column. Impacts to wildlife include 1300 dolphins, whales, and porpoises stranded along the Gulf coast, with 90 percent mortality. The endangered Kemp's Ridley Sea Turtle population has crashed from 50,000 to 11,000. Deep water reefs are dying, and crickets in coastal Louisiana have experienced a massive die off. The Deepwater Horizon spill came on the heels of the 1979 Ixtoc I spill, which was nearly as large. A great degree of uncertainty surrounds the Gulf Coast's future.

FRACKING

In a completely different sector, natural gas and petroleum extraction is now being performed in many areas using hydraulic fracturing, or fracking. Fracking is an unusual process developed to pull additional natural

"Frac job in process" by Joshua Doubek - Own work. Licensed under CC BY-SA 3.0 via Wikimedia Commons

COMPETITION FOR WATER IN U.S. SHALE ENERGY DEVELOPMENT

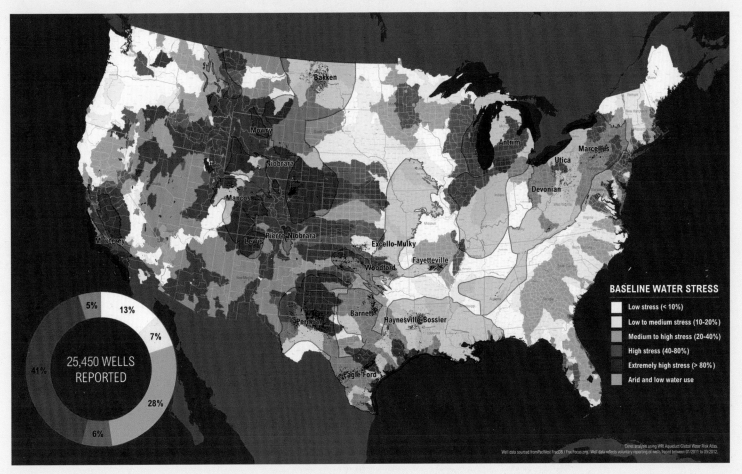

Map of hydraulically fractured well locations as overlaid onto the WRI's Aqueduct Water Risk Atlas using the baseline water risk indicator. Forty-seven percent of wells are found in regions with high or extremely high water risk indicating growing competitive pressure on water supplies for shale energy development. Well locations in the map above appear as black patches. The wells appear more clearly, as black circles, on the online map. Shale basins are represented by shaded areas.

gas out of the ground beyond what is extracted through natural pressure and/or conventional pumping. Fracking involves the injection of water, sand, and chemicals under very high pressure to release low density natural gas and allow it to flow to the well. At times, very large volumes of water are used. Sand is included in the mix to maintain the cracks opened during pressurization. The surface footprint of fracking is quite significant, including large tanks of water, large pumps, compressors, generators, and frequent truck deliveries of water and sand. Fracking has rapidly spread across North America, altering the face of many communities. Its negative impact is quite significant, including:

Air quality: During 2011, levels of smog in rural Wyoming exceeded that of Los Angeles due to fracking.

Earthquakes: According to the United States Geological Service,

Damage from the San Bruno pipeline explosion, which occurred on September 9, 2010, in San Bruno, CA, when a 30 inch steel natural gas pipeline exploded in flames. Photo: Thomas Hawk / Flickr Creative Commons

"Between the years 1973–2008, there was an average of twenty-one earthquakes of magnitude three and larger in the central and eastern United States. This rate jumped to an average of 99 M[agnitude] 3+ earthquakes per year in 2009–2013, and the rate continues to rise." The increase in tectonic destabilization is entirely attributable to fracking. Larger scaled earthquakes caused by fracking, including in 2011 in Prague, Oklahoma (magnitude 5.6), in Trinidad, Colorado (magnitude 5.3), in Guy, Arkansas (magnitude 4.7), and in 2012 in Timpson, Texas, (magnitude 4.8), are beginning to occur.

Drinking water contamination: In many areas, the extraction process has led to the contamination of well water, particularly where shallower fracking is performed.

Intensive water use: According to Ceres, Nearly half (47 percent) of oil and gas wells recently hydraulically fractured in the United States are in regions with high or extremely high water stress. Between January

"The U.S. Pipeline and Hazardous Materials Safety Administration database has tracked 916 serious pipeline incidents since 1995, resulting in 365 deaths and 1,405 injuries in the United States alone. In Nigeria, the toll has been much larger, with about 3,000 killed in eleven explosions since 1998."

2011 and May 2013, fracking in the United States used 97 billion gallons of water, about the equivalent used by Salt Lake City and its suburbs for a four year period.

Habitat degradation: Fracking and natural gas wells are destroying the boreal forests of northwest Canada. Canada is home to nearly 25 percent of intact forests worldwide.

Truck traffic: The average fracking well requires four hundred truckloads of water and up to twenty-five railcars of sand delivered. The Pennsylvania Department of Transportation recently determined that it would take $265 million to repair roads damaged by fracking.

Methane release: Per pound, methane has 84 times the heat retention capacity of CO_2. Natural gas and methane leakage is a significant contributor to climate change, and is often not considered in overall greenhouse gas counts. According to the Environmental Defense Fund, the impact of this leakage within the United States is equal to the emissions of half the cars in the United States — a stunning amount.

Explosion: In a two year period beginning in July 2013, North America experienced ten tanker rail car explosions, commencing with a major derailment and explosion in Lac-Mégantic,

Quebec, where 53 people were killed. The train originated from Bakken Formation oil in North Dakota, and was headed to New Brunswick for refinement. A 2014 Wall Street Journal study found that Bakken oil was three times more explosive than typical crude. This oil is now being transported throughout North America.

Pipeline explosions are even more commonplace, with particularly deadly consequences in the developing world. The U.S. Pipeline and Hazardous Materials Safety Administration database has tracked 916 serious pipeline incidents since 1995, resulting in 365 deaths and 1,405 injuries in the United States alone. In Nigeria, the toll has been much larger, with about 3,000 killed in eleven explosions since 1998.

This litany is both relentless and real. Any one of these impacts should be enough to prompt action and, in aggregate, a major cultural, technological, and institutional shift. Discussing these things at length is done here to answer the "why?" of net zero energy. Net zero practitioners are engaged in a critical, even sacred effort to change our society to limit harm to ourselves and the planet. It is to that story that we now turn.

PART II

NET ZERO PROJECTS

THE SEARCH
FOR EFFICIENCY

So, how is this level of efficiency achieved, let alone be possible? At the meta level, it takes both great creativity and great analysis — the left and right brains, hand in hand. Close reading of baseline energy usage and energy modeling must be carefully performed, all the while staying fresh and loose to think of new ways of doing things and maintaining perspective. Giving time to think about the building both in evolutionary and revolutionary terms will yield a powerful, well functioning design.

Perhaps the best starting point is for the design team to ask very fundamental questions about what they are designing and where they are designing it. What will really happen in the building? Who will be in it? What will they be doing? Could they be doing something else? To design highly efficient buildings, an excellent question to ask is: Is it necessary? If it is not, perhaps it should not be there. Equally critical then is a consideration of designing with nature, biophilia, and biomimetics: what is happening on the site? What of the four Greek elements that come to the site — earth, wind, fire, and water — and how can they be used beneficially?

After fundamental reference points are established, it is then appropriate to determine how a similar building (type and climate) to that being designed typically uses energy. Typically, this is done by simply finding good baseline examples of similar buildings and using either actual submetering data, or estimates, to outline the energy uses

SHOEBOX MODEL

Graphic: PAE Engineering

Shoebox model wireframe for new Rocky Mountain Institute Snowmass Headquarters, registered for Net Zero Energy Building certification

Legend:
- Ext. Usage
- Domestic Hot Water
- HT Pump Supplem.
- Refrig. Display
- Vent Fans
- Pumps & Aux
- Heat Reject
- Space Cooling
- Space Heating
- Plug Loads
- Task Lights
- Lights

Chart y-axis: kBtu/sf/year (0–80)

X-axis categories: Baseline Building, REDUCED INFILTRATION, INCREASED WALL INS, INCREASED ROOF INS, HIGH PERFORMANCE GLAZING, INCREASED FLOOR INS, MASS FLOOR, DECREASED LPD, DAYLIGHTING, HEAT RECOVERY, DEMAND CONTROLLED VENTILATION, INCREASED VENTILATION, INTERACTIVE WITH CODE VENTILATION, INTERACTIVE WITH INCREASED VENTILATION, ALL IN 20% NORTH GLAZING, ALL IN 30% NORTH GLAZING, DESCRIPTION OF MODEL

TYPICAL COMMERCIAL OFFICE BUILDING EUI

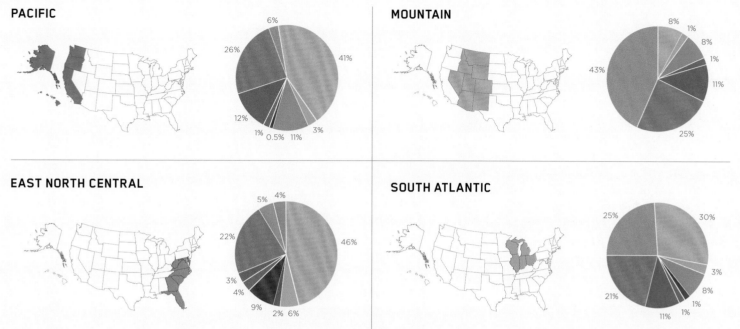

PACIFIC

MOUNTAIN

EAST NORTH CENTRAL

SOUTH ATLANTIC

This graphic shows typical EUI's for commercial office buildings in different climate zones. Building energy use can be influenced by a number of factors including climate, design, building operations and maintenance practices, and occupant behavior. End energy use can vary significantly in different climates. Note that while the Portland, Phoenix, and Atlanta average EUIs are nearly the same, the way energy is used varies due to climate, with Phoenix using significantly more cooling and ventilation due to very hot temperatures, and almost no heating. Chicago has a higher EUI because it is both very hot in the summer and very cold in the winter.

at the sector level of the building — heating, cooling, ventilation, hot water, user loads, and so on. It is important to not overly focus on this data, because the building will hopefully be designed with a fresh eye to the future, and not rely on how things have been done in the past. It is, however, a useful starting point in understanding what sorts of needs and demands are confronted by the design team. However, if the building design process simply ends up being an exercise in

load reduction, the best design may not be achieved, and creative, cost-effective ideas and techniques missed. At this point the design team typically will use a basic modeling program to evaluate the efficacy of different design approaches, called a "shoebox" model. This modeling allows basic order of magnitude analyses.

There are several conceptual frames of focus for net zero energy buildings:

Natural vs. Mechanical: Some buildings may rely on thermal gain, wind or thermal ventilation, or natural daylight to achieve conservation. Others may rely on high-efficiency mechanized systems. Natural building systems tend to require more deliberate design, are more durable (because typically they are an inherent part of the building structure), and also are more biophilic — the nature of the light, heat, cool, and air all tend to vary within these buildings.

DESIGNING FOR RESILIENCE

A great side benefit of net zero energy buildings, only somewhat explored to date, is that they are inherently resilient, particularly in terms of thermal performance. Alex Wilson, President of the Resilient Design Institute and founder of Building Green, Inc., has developed the idea of "drift temperature", which is the internal temperature of a building when it has no powered inputs. In a significant long-term emergency, when no power is available, does the building still provide the fundamentals of shelter? Most net zero energy buildings, with their typically excellent thermal envelopes, may stay quite habitable, say in the 50s F and even 60s F, even when it is subfreezing outside. This is due to thermal gain through windows, and retention through the shell. For example, during an ice storm and associated power outage, lack of power may be a real crisis in a typical building, which can drop below freezing, resulting in danger to its occupants, systems, and structure. In the meantime, the net zero energy building may not be completely comfortable, but at least it will be much more habitable.

While design for net zero energy typically results in buildings with a good drift temperature, paying particular attention to this question is worthwhile as a stand-alone side effort, and may result in changes in design which would not otherwise emerge. Modeling drift temperature performance in particular may result in changes to window placement and specification to increase wintertime thermal gain. Certainly an orientation to resiliency and drift temperature tends to favor passive and envelope oriented strategies over mechanical systems. Decision making between passive and active systems should include resiliency in their tradeoff considerations.

Mechanical systems allow more flexibility. Many buildings create an interesting hybrid of the two.

Building envelope vs. internal systems: Many net zero energy buildings work very hard at retaining heat and cool internally, through very high levels of insulation and very thorough air sealing. Others may focus more on highly efficient mechanical systems. In actuality, in most climate zones, both are needed to achieve net zero energy performance. A heavy focus on improving the envelope has the significant advantage of being an inherent part of the building, while mechanical systems may only last 15-20 years. However, very high levels of insulation and sealing is not necessarily less expensive per watt saved relative to mechanical systems. In addition, in a retrofit scenario where a deep renovation is involved, mechanical systems can provide very cost-effective ways to radically reduce energy use.

Tested vs. prototypic: Reassuringly, most designs and technologies used in net zero energy buildings have been used in a variety of settings. However, at times approaches which are less familiar, or even completely new may be considered. It is important for team members to be aware of any risks associated with their design, and the project's capacity for uncertainty. Many NZE projects will introduce a design innovation or two, which helps to build the building science legacy for the future.

Parallel to the process of designing a highly efficient building, project teams should evaluate the potential sources of renewable energy — solar electric, wind, solar hot water, small scale hydroelectric, etcetera. While the significant majority of NZEB Certified projects use solar electric generation, it is appropriate to evaluate other alternatives — while most parts of the world do not have enough wind for viable wind generation, those that do may be a good candidate. Having a deep understanding of solar access to the site — shade, solar angles, availability during various times of the year and so on will give the team a deeper understanding of how much is available.

As project teams evolve their designs, alternative layouts and designs may be vetted which handle various elements differently. More specialized modeling, including computational fluid dynamics which evaluate air flow and wind

"It is critical for net zero energy projects to have an overall leader and champion, who bridges the disciplines, can question and push, and maintain perspective and vision."

zHome – Five of ten homes certified as Net Zero Energy Buildings.

33

across the building, may be employed. An evaluation of trade offs between different systems, focusing on cost and also accounting for an array of characteristics, often comes into play.

During the zHome design process, two alternative heating/hot water systems were qualitatively evaluated not only for cost but an array of other considerations. While one may or may not agree with the scoring, this is a helpful example of a design team grappling with making decisions.

One very important element of effective achievement of net zero energy, indeed any project, is leadership, decision making, and maintaining the big picture. It is critical for net zero energy projects to have an overall leader and champion, who bridges the disciplines, can question and push, and maintain perspective and vision. Even the best experts will have blind spots, crises will arise, and thousands of decisions will be made. An effective leader will understand every detail, the role of each person on the team,

and be a good troubleshooter. This role, often underestimated, is critical for the success of achieving ultimate net zero energy performance.

Again, this section is not meant to be a full how-to manual of good design, but rather it is to provide key points and tips on effectively achieving net zero energy performance. We now turn to fifteen real projects which have gone through a design and decision-making process to achieve exactly that, offering an inspiring vision for a carbon free future.

GETTING TO NET ZERO ENERGY – DESIGN PROCESS

Achieving net zero energy performance draws from the key adages mentioned above, such as a penny saved is a penny earned, living within your means, and reaping the harvest. Net zero energy begins with reducing energy use as much as possible — radically — and then finding on-site renewables to offset that use. This section is not meant to be an all inclusive manual of design or integrated process. Rather, it is meant to provide examples of specific methods, considerations, and mindsets useful for achieving a very difficult performance goal.

To set expectations for conservation up front, the energy use per square foot reduction is significant in each of the case studies which follow, ranging from 50 percent to 80 percent savings. In other words, to achieve net zero energy, the entire building must be rethought, and every watt of energy potentially used must be considered. This level of conservation is generally physically necessary to achieve net zero energy, due to limitations on available photovoltaic (PV) placement on rooftops (PV is the most typical energy production source on NZEB Certified buildings). The attached series of graphics of the Bullitt Center shows the relative size of needed solar offset based on differing levels of Energy Use Intensity. Clearly, significant reductions are needed to bring the overall energy use to a point where there is enough physical space to provide an offset.

A typical building of this size has an Energy Use Intensity of 72 kBtu/sf/yr. A PV array with an area of 63,348 sf is required to meet its energy needs.

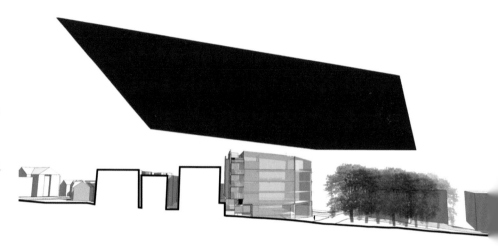

A typical building of this size has an Energy Use Intensity of 51 kBtu/sf/yr. A PV array with an area of 44,752 sf is required to meet its energy needs.

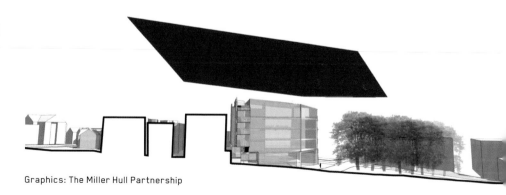

Graphics: The Miller Hull Partnership

A typical building of this size has an Energy Use Intensity of 32 kBtu/sf/yr. A PV array with an area of 28,599 sf is required to meet its energy needs.

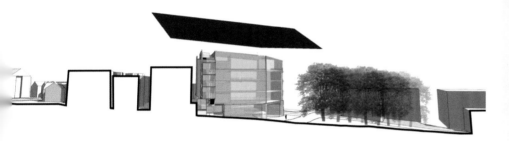

A typical building of this size has an Energy Use Intensity of 16 kBtu/sf/yr. A PV array with an area of 14,303 sf is required to meet its energy needs.

ENERGY USE INTENSITY (EUI) AND REVEAL

Energy Use Intensity (EUI) is the amount of energy use per square foot for a building. Within the United States, EUI is measured in units of 1,000 British Thermal Units (kBtu) per square foot per year – not necessarily the most intuitive measure. In metric based countries, EUI is measured in units of 1,000 watt hours (kWh) per square meter per year.

In 2015, the ILFI launched Reveal, a third party certification for EUI performance. This certification program, in its pilot phase at the time of publication of this book, is meant to highlight the most efficient buildings in each category and climate zone.

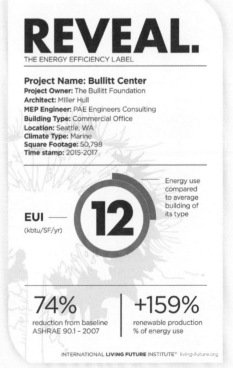

REVEAL.
THE ENERGY EFFICIENCY LABEL

Project Name: Bullitt Center
Project Owner: The Bullitt Foundation
Architect: Miller Hull
MEP Engineer: PAE Engineers Consulting
Building Type: Commercial Office
Location: Seattle, WA
Climate Type: Marine
Square Footage: 50,798
Time stamp: 2015-2017

EUI ——
(kbtu/SF/yr)

12

Energy use compared to average building of its type

74%
reduction from baseline ASHRAE 90.1 - 2007

+159%
renewable production % of energy use

INTERNATIONAL **LIVING FUTURE** INSTITUTE™ living-future.org

RESIDENTIAL

BUILDINGS

zHOME

ISSAQUAH, WA, USA

PROJECT TEAM

OWNER, DEVELOPER, AND GENERAL CONTRACTOR:
Ichijo USA

ARCHITECT:
David Vandervort Architects

CIVIL ENGINEER:
Core Design

MECHANICAL ENGINEER:
Stantec

STRUCTURAL ENGINEER:
Harriott Valentine Engineers

ELECTRICAL ENGINEER:
Bennett Electrical

PLUMBING ENGINEER:
Stantec

GEOTECHNICAL CONSULTANT:
Icicle Creek

INTERIOR DESIGN:
LH Design and Patti Southard

LIGHTING DESIGN:
Seattle Lighting

LANDSCAPE ARCHITECT:
Darwin Webb Landscape Architects

SPECIALTY CONSULTANTS:
WSP, 2020 Engineering, Northwest Wind and Solar

SUBCONTRACTORS:
Northwest Mechanical, Northwest Wind and Solar

SIZE:
10 homes / 13,401 sf total

BUILDING FOOTPRINT:
5,812 sf

SITE:
17,179 sf

TYPE:
Residential, Educational (one unit used as education center)

LIVING TRANSECT:
L4, General Urban Zone

WEBSITE:
z-home.org/outline.php

LOCATION:
Issaquah, WA, USA

EUI:
17.5 - 20.6 kBtu/sf/year for homes, 17.5 kBtu/sf/year for Stewardship Center (education, event, office space).

PV SIZE:
3 kW

OTHER RENEWABLES:
None

CLIMATE ZONE:
Marine

ANNUAL ENERGY USE:
ACTUAL: 3,012 kWh
SIMULATED/DESIGNED: N/A

CONSTRUCTION COST:
$226/sf

CERTIFICATION:
ILFI-certified Net Zero Energy Building for five of ten homes as well as community energy uses

DATES CERTIFIED:
May 2013; September 2015

The zHome project was launched in 2006 as a market catalyst for deeply sustainable, climate neutral homes for everyday people. Born out of the context of years of small increments of improvement in environmental performance in green building, the creators sought to revolutionize the paradigm for what was possible, creating hope and action within the context of cultural and political confusion and inaction regarding climate change, persistent toxicity, and overconsumption. The project was initially conceived by Brad Liljequist (lead author of this book) while on sabbatical from his role as green building and urban design consultant in 2005, during visits to the groundbreaking British restorative communities of BedZED and the Hockerton Housing Project, as well as the University of Nottingham Jubilee campus. The City of Issaquah, whose green building program Liljequist managed, had long been a regional leader in sustainability. The City was responsible for the first

LEED Silver building in the State of Washington, and was well known for its pioneering waste reduction programs. For Issaquah, one of the fastest growing cities in the state (more than 1,000 homes a year for much of the 2000s), reducing the environmental impact of its new construction was a major priority.

The City led a coalition of local partners, including Built Green, Ichijo USA, King County, Puget Sound Energy, and the Washington State University Energy Office to bring the project to fruition as a regional catalyst for net zero energy action. In addition to the net zero energy target for the project, zHome also included an array of cutting edge environmental targets (although short of the Living Building Challenge). These initiatives included a 70 percent reduction in water use through rainwater reuse, and the replication of the predevelopment site hydrology through a sophisticated set of rain gardens and infiltration systems. Additionally, 80 percent of all wood used in project construction was FSC-certified.

Sale of the homes occurred in 2012 and 2013, just as the area was recovering from the economic downturn. The project has undergone two phases of certification. The first, finalized in April 2014, certified the performance of the Stewardship Center, one of the ten homes which was used as an education, event, and office space, the community loads of the project, which were substantial as they included the large ground source wellfield pumps, and the first unit to achieve twelve months of performance data. The second certification, performed in September of 2015 as this book was finalized, evaluated eight of the ten zHome units. Through this second certification, three additional units were certified as NZE homes. Three units did not achieve net zero energy performance, and two of the units did not provide permission for the release of energy use data by the local utility, Puget Sound Energy. It is hoped that the remaining homes will be certified as they achieve net zero energy performance.

DEVELOPMENT AND FINANCING

zHome was made possible by a highly innovative and complex development arrangement that involved several organizations. zHome was built in Issaquah Highlands, an urban village developed by Port Blakely Communities on the outskirts of Issaquah. The City desired the construction of zHome as well as the development of a partner affordable housing community, the YWCA Family Village. The City brokered a four-way land transfer deal whereby Port Blakely transferred the zHome and Family Village sites to the developers at no cost in exchange for several revisions to its Issaquah Highlands development agreement. The zHome developer received the land in exchange for paying the City's management costs, covering the developer's significantly increased management and design fees, use of one of the 10 zHome units as an education center for five years, and absorbing the risk associated with building a prototype for an untested market. Unfortunately, the two initial zHome development partners were forced to pull out of the project because of the financial downturn (the original project "groundbreaking" occurred on September 29, 2007—the day the Dow Jones Industrial dropped 777 points). As the U.S. economy recovered, a new joint venture was formed with Ichijo, the second largest home builder in Japan, which was entering the U.S. market and interested in producing carbon neutral housing. While the original project was anticipated to be financed through typical bank financing, this was no longer available because of the financial conditions of the time. The end result was that Ichijo self-financed construction of the project. A core benchmark of zHome was that the additional costs to achieve the environmental benchmarks would not exceed 20 percent above typical area townhome costs. Due to the nature of the development arrangement, which made it difficult to assess the true construction costs of zHome, a replication financial pro forma was put together which reflected the costs if zHome was built without the extraneous elements of the development deal. This pro forma determined the construction cost per square foot (hard and soft costs, without land) would be $226/sf. Even within the context of the economic downturn, the sales prices of $350,000 to $600,000 meant that the 20 percent premium to achieve zHome's performance standard was recovered.

FINANCING

Soft costs:	$622,000
Hard costs:	$2,412,000
Price per square foot (hard and soft costs only):	$226/square foot
Public incentives (state, local, federal):	The value of the 30 percent tax credit for the photovoltaic array transferred to the homeowners at purchase. The State of Washington also has no sales tax on photovoltaic systems. Finally, the State of Washington also provides a $0.15/kwh production incentive for each kilowatt of solar energy produced through 2020. This incentive will also be passed on to the homeowners.
Private sources:	Ichijo USA self-financed the project. Homes were sold at market rate. The City of Issaquah provided the land as an incentive to Ichijo USA; however, most of the value of the land was offset by contractually obligated project expenses.
TOTAL PROJECT COST (excluding land purchase):	**$3,034,000**

SITE CONTEXT
AND CLIMATE ZONE

zHome is located within Issaquah Highlands, a major neotraditional urban village built as part of a designated urban growth area adjacent to the City of Issaquah. Issaquah itself is one of the older communities in the central Puget Sound, incorporated in 1892, just three years after Washington's Statehood. Issaquah Highlands was designed around smart growth principles, and is known for its highly walkable, textured urban design. zHome is located on the edge of the Highland's town center, and is a block from a King County regional transit center.

zHome is located in the DOE temperate climate zone, the same one as the Bullitt Center and several other projects in this book. However, there is significant variation in climate zones. Issaquah, only about ten miles east of Seattle, sits in the middle of the Issaquah Alps, the first foothills of the Cascade Mountains. Annual rainfall is about ten inches more per year, and wintertime temperatures are frequently five to ten degrees cooler than Seattle. During the winter, snow often occurs in the Issaquah Highlands while Seattle is snow free. Finding a good long-term, data set for Issaquah was challenging, since weather stations tended to be located closer to the Puget Sound's tempering effect. The design team factored this variation into its modeling, but there was some uncertainty.

EUI: zHOME

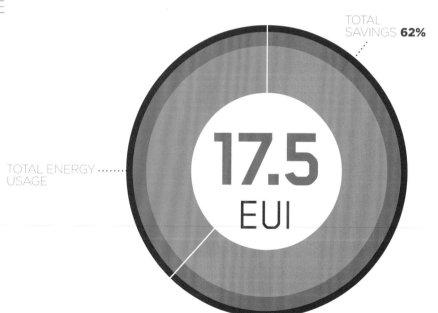

TOTAL SAVINGS **62%**

TOTAL ENERGY USAGE

17.5
EUI

62%
SAVINGS FROM BASELINE

46
KBTU/SF/YEAR BASELINE EUI*

* RECS 2009,
single family detached
general climate category

43

ENERGY STORY: ACHIEVING NET ZERO AND BEYOND

Conceptual design: zHome was explicitly designed from its beginning (2006) with a core design benchmark targeting net zero energy. This ambitious benchmark defined net zero energy as "...the occupants will need to purchase no more 'standard purchased energy' (defined below) than the project will generate, and introduce onto the public electric grid via surplus 'project renewable electrical sources' (defined below) over the course of one year...". Designing and building to this benchmark became a contractual obligation from the

builder (acting as developer) and the city (acting as zHome lead sponsor).

Design started in 2007, and a core team devoted to achieving the net zero energy goal included the mechanical engineer Tom Marseille, then with Stantec, now with WSP; Chuck Murray, residential energy code lead for the State of Washington; Mark Weirenga, project architect; Dennis Rominger, project manager for the builder; and Brad Liljequist, overall project manager. The team established a design approach of achieving net

zero energy performance at the least cost, but also addressing a number of other design considerations, including:

- Constructability/Replicability
- Noise Reduction
- Life Cycle Cost/Durability
- Complexity/Maintainability
- Ability to Retrofit/Flexibility
- Health and Toxicity

There was an extended period of conceptual design, using a basic "shoebox" energy model for assisting with design, evaluated envelope, passive and active systems for achieving net zero energy. A baseline case energy usage for typical 1-, 2-, and 3-bedroom Issaquah area townhomes was established.

PART II: NET ZERO PROJECTS

wind speed of just under 4 mph, the site's wind production was determined to not be cost effective and, as a result, on-site solar photovoltaic energy production was selected. On the energy demand side, it was clear (based on the initial shoebox model) that focusing on reducing heating and hot water loads would be key to solving zHome's net zero energy challenge. Over the course of a number of meetings about twenty varied options were identified as possible system designs. These were further winnowed to a fundamental envelope of R-38 walls and R-60 roof, U-.30 windows, an ACH static air leakage rate (of the home) of .20, and two different heating/hot water options: (1) a ground source heat pump, and (2) an air source heat pump coupled with solar hot water and a natural gas cold temperature boiler.

These systems were approximately cost equivalent, and based on the qualitative criteria the ground source heat pump system was selected for its relative simplicity, no on-site combustion, and lower maintenance. A heat recovery ventilator rounds out the system fundamentals.

The wild card in the energy use profile was the user. As a final component of the initial analysis, using Department of Energy residential plug load studies, the team projected reasonable plug load demands for residents motivated

The team began its work by identifying the preferred energy generation for the project and its cost, based on the understanding that energy production was likely to be the most expensive aspect of achieving net zero energy. Based on the cost per watt of energy produced, a baseline "price" per energy saved on the building systems could be effectively evaluated—essentially, if energy savings on the demand side were more cost effective than the on-site renewable energy

production price, it made sense to proceed. (This design approach is less valid than it was at the time due to significant drops in solar prices). An anemometer was stationed at the nearby King County Park & Ride to evaluate wind power potential in the immediate vicinity and interpolated to a nearby weather station in Issaquah Highlands, as well as to the National Oceanic and Atmospheric Administration (NOAA) observations to evaluate wind flows. At an average to efficiently use energy within the context of living in a net zero energy residence. In tandem with a real-time energy use monitor, phantom load wall switches, and education, the team thought that there was a good chance the residents would do their part to lower their energy draw.

The energy model then finalized the full demand side assumptions of each unit and assessed the size of the solar electric system needed to offset the usage on an annualized basis. The expected size of the system and rough dimensions on each rooftop were evaluated to ensure there would be adequate roof area for the systems. (There was, with room to spare.) This initial energy model was then summarized and peer reviewed by the WSU Energy Office acting on behalf of the zHome partnership. In practice, energy usage was higher than projected. This was offset by higher than modeled photovoltaic performance.

The site design itself also reduces the prominence of the automobile and encourages low carbon mobility options. Community garages are maintained at the north edge of the site, and microvehicle head in parking is located along the adjacent street. The first public electric vehicle charging stations in the Seattle metro Eastside area are placed by the microvehicle parking as well.

DESIGN ELEMENTS

Building envelope: The building envelope is comprised of the following elements:
R-38 Walls: Two inch by six inch wood framing with a combination of expanded polystyrene and mineral wool was used as infill insulation. Additionally, 3.25 inches of continuous expanded polystyrene was used outside the sheathed wall. One issue that arose during construction was that the proposed Hardiepanel was warrantable with only one inch of exterior insulation maximum. The project team worked with the Hardie Corporation to create a specification that would allow warranting of a much thicker section of insulation using a combination of lag screws and 1"x4" rainscreen lath.
R-60 Ceiling: Two SIP-like panelized sections were used, one 2"x8" and one 2"x10" stacked atop each other, using standard wood framing. Cavities were filled with tightly fit, expanded polystyrene. Framing stud locations were offset to create a discontinuous thermal bridge created by the studs.
R-10 Under slab: This is provided by expanded polystyrene.
U-.30 maximum windows: Double-pane low-E, argon filled Pella fiberglass windows were used. A sensitivity analysis was performed assessing the use of triple-pane windows which were determined to not be cost effective due to the minimal incremental benefit once other measures had been applied.

Each zHome has its own heat pump and hot water storage tank

Static pressure 0.20 air changes per hour: Supported by Tom Balderston of Conservation Services Group, the team used a blower door test to assess and reduce air leakage locations at various points during construction and achieved the target 0.20 air changes per hour as a minimum air leakage rate.

Heating and hot water: zHome used a common ground loop heat exchanger "wellfield" for all ten units consisting of fifteen 220 foot deep vertical boreholes. These were circulated in a head-balanced system with two large Grundfos pumps. Each unit has its own sidefeed and return to this field. Within each unit, an individual Water Furnace heat pump is provided that feeds heated water to a storage tank which provides domestic hot water storage and, via heat exchange, heated water. Heat distribution to spaces is provided through in-floor hydronic tubing under concrete slab and bamboo flooring.

zHOME SITE PLAN

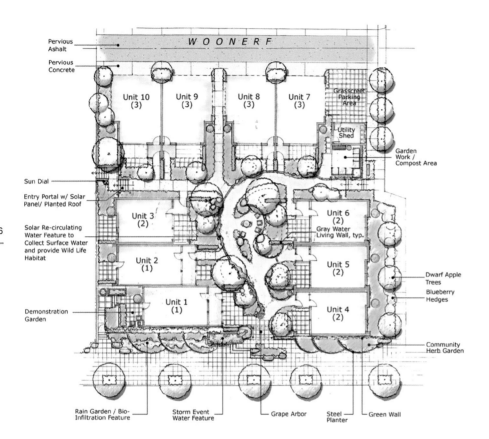

Pervious Asphalt
Pervious Concrete
WOONERF
Unit 10 (3)
Unit 9 (3)
Unit 8 (3)
Unit 7 (3)
Grasscreet Parking Area
Utility Shed
Garden Work / Compost Area
Sun Dial
Entry Portal w/ Solar Panel/ Planted Roof
Solar Re-circulating Water Feature to Collect Surface Water and provide Wild Life Habitat
Unit 3 (2)
Unit 6 (2)
Gray Water Living Wall, typ.
Unit 2 (1)
Unit 5 (2)
Demonstration Garden
Unit 1 (1)
Unit 4 (2)
Dwarf Apple Trees
Blueberry Hedges
Community Herb Garden
Rain Garden / Bio-Infiltration Feature
Storm Event Water Feature
Grape Arbor
Steel Planter
Green Wall

OTHER KEY DEMAND SIDE CONSERVATION FEATURES

Heat recovery ventilation: Each home is equipped with a Lifebreath heat recovery ventilator which provides tempered fresh air into the space.

Natural cooling ventilation: Each home was designed with an open layout between floors and a high opening clerestory to provide natural summertime evening ventilation through stack effect when the low and high windows are opened. This works particularly well, especially on the taller units.

Energy feedback monitors: Energy Detective energy monitors are provided in each unit.

Phantom load switched outlets: Black colored outlets and switches are paired to allow phantom load generating appliances to be easily switched off.

Deep daylighting: Extensive consideration was given to daylight in the project design, including a high volume main space with a north facing clerestory.

LED and fluorescent lighting: There is no incandescent lighting in the project.

Highly energy-efficient appliances: Top of the range Energy Star certified appliances include GE refrigerators, Fridgedaire clothes washers and dryers, Bosch dishwashers, and Samsung induction ranges.

Renewables: Each zHome unit has its own array modeled to offset the anticipated energy use within the home. Based on unit size, the one, two, and three bedroom units have 4.8, 6, and 7 kWh arrays, respectively. The system uses Solarworld 240 watt panels coupled with Enphase 190 DC-AC microinverters. The microinverters allow soiled or otherwise underfunctioning panels to be isolated from the rest of the solar circuit. Electricity from the panels flows through a production meter and then to a net meter administered by Puget Sound Energy.

CONSTRUCTION PROCESS AND CONSTRUCTABILITY ISSUES

A particularly difficult phase of zHome's construction was the drilling of the ground source borehole field. Issaquah Highlands sits on a glacial lateral moraine and abuts a former gravel quarry. While drainage is excellent, the sand and the gravel surrounding the boreholes frequently collapsed, making drilling extremely challenging. As a result, construction was delayed by over a month. Because the units were for-sale townhomes, it was determined that buyer expectations required each home to have its own heating/hot water system. The smallest heat pump that was available was far larger than was actually required, and to avoid short cycling of the heat pump, a very large (120 gallon) water tank was also needed. The result was the overbuilding of the heat pump system, that also necessitated a large amount of space relative to the overall home sizes. In retrospect, a single heat pump per building, combined with heat tanks in each home, would likely have sufficed.

Each zHome has its own rooftop array. Panels for community loads such as the ground source wellfield pumps are dispersed over all the rooftops.

47

OCCUPANCY: ZHOME IN REAL LIFE

zHome is now fully occupied with nine families in nine homes and one stewardship/education center in the tenth. At the time of the first phase of Net Zero Energy Building certification, only the Stewardship Center and one zHome unit had been occupied for a full year. In addition, the community infrastructure system had also been in operation for over a year. All three of these homes/systems achieved net zero energy over the course of the year and were thus certified. The second phase of certification, as mentioned above, resulted in a total of five homes and the community system certified at net zero energy performance. Of the remaining homes, three have not performed at net zero energy, and permission for review of energy performance was not obtained for the other two.

NZEB

This graph shows 12 month energy performance for 14 consecutive periods with start dates beginning in March 2013 and ending in May 2014. It shows the reality of net zero energy over time – some homes are solidly net zero energy for all 14 months, while another barely makes it for one.

ENERGY CONSUMPTION

This graph shows just energy usage during the same observation periods – one gratifying observation is that, in general, energy usage over time is going down, suggesting that the residents are refining their occupancy over time. Another important thing to note is that even the worst performing home in the worst performing period still only uses less than a net 2,500 kwh annually – a small fraction of the baseline energy use of a typical area townhome of 16,000 kwh/year – demonstrating the power of NZE buildings as a key response to reducing energy use.

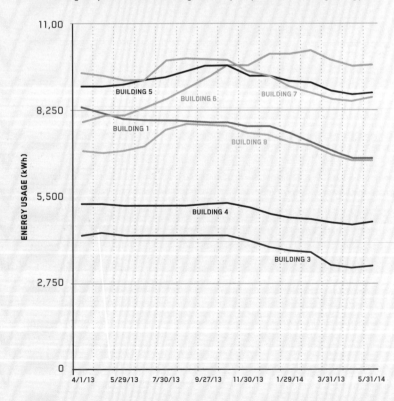

Part of the national marketing launch for the Mitsubishi i-Miev electric vehicle was held at zHome.

ZHOME'S LOCAL LEGACY

zHome is a terrific example of a relatively small-scale project having significant impact, on a number of fronts. zHome was intended as a demonstration of hope about climate change and environmental problems in a practical, accessible way, and also included an in-depth regional education outreach program. Over the course of nine weekends, more than 10,000 people visited the project and received an in-depth educational tour from a team of volunteer docents. In addition, over one hundred technical classes involving 5,000 engineers, architects, and designers were given about the project and its systems. Classes were also given during construction to technical and professional audiences. zHome also left a local legacy of follow-on, deeply energy efficient projects. After completing zHome, the City of Issaquah built the Maple Street Fire Station, the world's most energy efficient fire station, which won the international ASHRAE Technology Award. About a half mile from zHome, the Swedish Medical Center was built as one of the most energy efficient hospitals worldwide, with an observed EUI of 108 kBtu/sf. The Ichijo construction company later built several homes performing at or near net zero energy. This company has adopted a standard specification for all homes which reduces energy use by half of what is required by building code, as well as including a three kilowatt solar array. While none of these initiatives are a direct result of zHome, the project did establish a legacy of expectation for deep energy performance within the local community and beyond.

WILLOWBROOK HOUSE

AUSTIN, TX, USA

PROJECT TEAM

OWNERS AND DESIGNERS:
Sunshine and Emily Mathon

MECHANICAL ENGINEER:
RM Mechanical

SOLAR ELECTRIC:
Lighthouse Solar

SOLAR HOT WATER:
Techsun

SPRAY FOAM:
Hill Country Insulation

EXTERIOR R-ETRO INSULATION:
Green Oaks

CONSTRUCTION MANAGER:
Shiloh Travis

SIZE:
2 floors / 2,100 sf

BUILDING FOOTPRINT:
2,100 sf

SITE:
9,044 sf

TYPE:
Residential Building

LIVING TRANSECT:
L3, Village or Campus Zone

WEBSITE:
living-future.org/case-study/willowbrook-house

LOCATION:
Austin, TX, USA

EUI:
8.59 kBtu/ft/yr

PV SIZE:
4.5kW DC (18 250W panels + micro inverters)

OTHER RENEWABLES:
Solar thermal hot water (2 roof panels + 80 gallon storage)

CLIMATE ZONE:
Hot-Humid

ANNUAL ENERGY USE:
ACTUAL: 5,310 kWh

CONSTRUCTION COST:
$186/sf

CERTIFICATION:
ILFI-certified Net Zero Energy Building

DATE CERTIFIED:
May 2014

Set on a slope above the street frontage, the Willowbrook House in Austin, Texas is one of the most energy efficient residential structures in the United States. Originally built in 1948, in a post-WWII neighborhood with a mid-century flair, this ILFI-Certified Net Zero Certified Building is the 2,100 square foot residence of a family of four. Purchased for $251,000, the structure underwent a deep remodel retrofit to achieve net zero performance. The owners, Sunshine and Emily Mathon, sought a larger home for their growing family and located the perfect site to achieve their vision for a home that produced enough energy to sustain itself. Materials and water were also important elements of the project, focusing on reclaimed wood and water efficiency. Greywater reuse was considered for the site; however, regulatory issues prevented the installation of a greywater system.

ENERGY STORY: ACHIEVING NET ZERO AND BEYOND

The existing house was highly inefficient, comprised of a concrete block envelope with no insulation, single-paned steel framed windows, and a poorly insulated attic with an HVAC system in a space that reached over 160 degrees during summer months. From an energy perspective, three existing elements helped shape the Willowbrook House into a Net Zero Energy home: a well chosen solar orientation, functional roof overhangs for shading, and the thermal mass of the concrete block exterior. All of these elements were optimized to create an efficient, comfortable, solar-powered home.

EUI: WILLOWBROOK HOUSE

TOTAL ENERGY USAGE ·········

TOTAL SAVINGS **78%**

8.59
EUI

78%
SAVINGS FROM BASELINE

39.1
KBTU/SF/YEAR BASELINE EUI*

* RECS 2009,
Hot humid residential
single family category

DESIGN ELEMENTS

Envelope: The original house's concrete block envelope had close to no thermal insulation. After a period of research, Quad Lock's R-ETRO interlocking EPS foam insulation blocks were chosen for the exterior of the concrete structure. These R-18 4-¼" foam blocks dramatically increased the building's efficiency. The addition was framed with wood and designed to maximize the use of insulation and minimize the use of a frame by using 2"x4" studs filled with open cell spray foam (R-12.6) and sheathed with ZIP R-panels. These panels include an additional sheet of polyiso insulation (R-3.3) laminated to the interior side of the sheathing, providing a thermal break to the wooden studs. The vaulted ceilings of the

FINANCING

Total project cost (excluding land purchase):	**$140,000**
Price with land and original house:	$251,000
Soft costs:	$15,000
Hard costs:	$125,000
PV system:	not available
Public incentives (state, local, federal):	Austin Energy's Value of Solar Tariff
Private sources:	None

addition follow the same methodology, but with greater insulation: R-6.6 of continuous polyicynene in addition to R-26 spray foam between 2"x8" rafters. The attic in the original portion of the home contains the air handler and ductwork and is sealed with 8 inches of open cellulose spray foam at the roof plane (R-28).

Heating/cooling: Heating and cooling for the house is provided by a 19-SEER, 9.5 HSPF Carrier Infinity Series 2-stage air-sourced heat pump. The heat pump is located in the attic, within the thermal envelope and air distribution occurs via new ducts installed throughout the house. The heating and cooling system is divided into three zones (living area, bedrooms and loft) with independent thermostat control and programming. Since the home is in a warm and humid climate, the system runs a dehumidification mode to take moisture out of the inside air during the spring and early summer. Fresh air is managed via a 150 cubic feet per minute (CFM) Fantec energy recovery ventilator (ERV). Large ceiling fans with induction motors efficiently cool spaces during warmer months. During the winter and summer, when heat or cooling is required and windows are rarely open, the ERV balances and pre-treats incoming fresh air with outgoing treated air, transferring heat and moisture. The ERV also acts as an exhaust for the bathrooms via a fan switch timer. In the spring and fall months, the heat pump and ERV are not frequently used, as the building's thermal mass and windows provide a comfortable operating temperature and ventilation. Overall, Sunshine Mathon believes that the existing high thermal mass of the concrete block, now located within the insulated envelope of the building, also provides a stabilizing influence on cooling demands even during hot periods.

Windows: During the remodel, the existing window openings were retained (given the concrete block construction) and fitted with Pella double-paned, fiberglass-framed windows with a U-value of 0.30.

THE POWER OF ZERO

The windows generally have a high Solar Heat Gain Coefficient (SHGC), so they are ideal for the warmer climate in Austin, but contain a different amount of SHGC shading based on their orientation in the house (allowing for more daylight).

PV system: The 4.5 kW (18 250W panels + micro inverters) DC array is mounted on the second-story addition loft metal standing seam roof. Attaching the solar electric array to a metal roof drastically reduced the number of roof penetrations and reduced the install cost for the solar electric by almost $1,000. The array is made up of eighteen 250 W Lumos monocrystalline panels mounted on S-5 standing seam clips and ProSolar Rooftrac racking with Enphase M215 microinverters. The inverters optimize energy production even when the roof is partially shaded by tree cover. Austin Energy provided a second meter showing consumption and production while also offering a "Value of Solar" credit, an advanced net-metering rate showing the ancillary costs the utility avoids with home-based systems. The house is monitored by an eGauge circuit level system and the high-load circuits in the house are individually monitored—a critical step in performance.

Solar hot water: The Willowbrook House features a solar hot water system, comprised of two Tinox Blue collectors which exchange heat in a closed loop system with stainless steel coils feeding to an 80-gallon water tank. The original hot water heater was located in the garage, so the new hot water closet was relocated to the center of the house (closer to the point of use), connecting the solar hot water panels on the loft roof. When a 10 degree temperature differential occurs, water is circulated through the system to collect the heat. When the water reaches a maximum temperature or sensors detect freezing, a separate pump removes the distilled water from the closed loop into a drainback tank mounted inside the thermal envelope of the hot water closet.

ZERO ENERGY HOUSE

AUCKLAND, NEW ZEALAND

The Zero Energy House (ZEH) is a 2,361 square foot certified Net Zero Energy Building in Auckland, New Zealand—the first of its kind in the country. Located on a brownfield site, the two-story structure features passive housing design, and was designed for comfort based on room use and building orientation. Design professionals Shay Brazier and Jo Woods are the owners of the house, which was largely personally financed as a home for their family.
Woods has an extensive background in materials science in engineering and Brazier is a highly experienced project leader with specific expertise in solar technologies. The bedrooms and living area of their home are positioned on the north side of the house for better solar exposure, whereas the kitchen and bathrooms occupy the south side of the lot. Adjacent to the living block is the play/work block, connected by an entryway featuring a workshop and garage. The pitched roof house takes the form of historic simplicity, evoking coastal California bungalows and the old state houses of New Zealand. The exterior is made up of unfinished Macrocarpa weatherboards giving the structure rustic detail. Reclaimed catamaran boat beams are used for the interior structure. The light finishes on the wood, large windows and concrete floors create a feeling of openness and brightness in the building space.

SIZE:
2 floors / 2,361 sf

BUILDING FOOTPRINT:
1,400 sf

SITE:
4,348 sf

TYPE:
Residential Building

LIVING TRANSECT:
L4, General Urban Zone

WEBSITE:
zeroenergyhouse.co.nz

LOCATION:
Auckland, New Zealand

57

EUI:
3.74 kBtu/sf/year

PV SIZE:
4.16kWp Photovoltaic array consisting of 88 x C21 roof tiles by SolarCity

OTHER RENEWABLES:
Eight Artline solar hot water collectors

CLIMATE ZONE:
Mixed Humid

ANNUAL ENERGY USE:
ACTUAL: 2,361 kWh
SIMULATED/DESIGNED: 3,217 kWh

CONSTRUCTION COST:
$193/sf

CERTIFICATION:
ILFI-certified Net Zero Energy Building

DATE CERTIFIED:
April 2014

ENERGY STORY: ACHIEVING NET ZERO AND BEYOND

The Zero Energy House (ZEH) is designed to achieve net zero energy over the course of the year through energy efficient features and solar energy systems. Innovative C21 PV roof slates, the first integrated PV system of its type in New Zealand, produce more energy than required to run the house. The building relies entirely on passive heating and cooling, the only certified Net Zero Energy Building to do so. To cover the slightly higher cost of the NZEB related systems, the owners reduced the overall size of the home by about 5 percent, that resulted in a house that cost the same net amount but with no energy cost.

FINANCING

TOTAL PROJECT COST (excluding land purchase):	**NZD $621,678** (approx. $518,065 USD)
Hard Cost:	NZD $553,355 (approx. $461,129 USD)
Soft Cost:	NZD $68,323 (approx. $56,936 USD)
PV system design: and installation	NZD $17,250 (approx. $14,375 USD)

ANNUAL ENERGY USE

HEATING + COOLING:
0 kWh

LIGHTING:
66 kWh or 0.33 kWh/sm/yr

FANS/PUMPS:
288 kWh or 1.44 kWh/m^2/yr

PLUG LOADS + EQUIPMENT:
888 kWh or 4.44 kWh/sm/yr

DOMESTIC HOT WATER:
222 kWh or 1.11 kWh/sm/yr

MONITORING AND CONTROL:
178 kWh or 0.89 kWh/sm/yr

REFRIGERATION:
356 kWh or 1.78 kWh/sm/yr

OVEN:
222 kWh or 1.11 kWh/m^2/yr

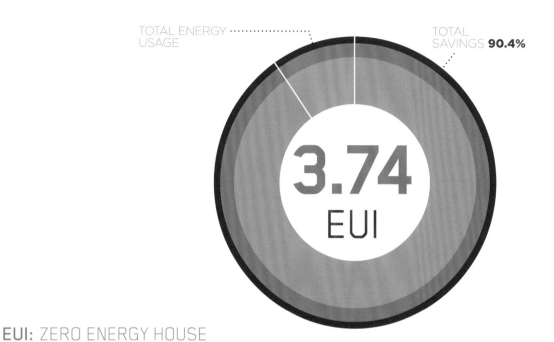

TOTAL ENERGY USAGE

TOTAL SAVINGS **90.4%**

3.74 EUI

90.4%
SAVINGS FROM BASELINE

39.1
KBTU/SF/YEAR
BASELINE EUI*

*RECS 2009,
Hot humid residential
single family category

EUI: ZERO ENERGY HOUSE

DESIGN ELEMENTS

Envelope: The climate in Auckland is relatively temperate, making typical high insulation strategies less necessary for good energy performance. Ninety millimeters wood framed walls are insulated with PET insulation, resulting in R-17. Windows are fairly typical low-E double-paned units.

Heating/cooling: The building is entirely passively heated and cooled. Careful attention to window placement and building overhangs enables thermal gain during cooler months while avoiding overheating during warm, humid months. Concrete flooring and thermal mass helps stabilize temperatures throughout the year.

Hot water: The Zero Energy House takes advantage of the north facing roof with the addition of eight roof integrated Artline flat plate collectors for the solar water heating system. These plates have been manufactured in Christchurch, NZ for over three decades, adding to the system's sustainable, local efforts. The system pumps water to the roof via a Grundfos PM2 solar circulator, heating it with solar energy, and returning hot water to the cylinder tank on the first floor of the house. The pump has varying speeds informed by temperature. To compensate for times when less solar energy is available, the pump operates at a slower speed, keeping water in the collectors for a longer period of time.

Renewables: The Zero Energy House features a roof integrated 4.16 kw photovoltaic array as a means to demonstrate the aesthetics of this innovative technology and the potential future of building products that incorporate PV cells as a building material. These

unique panels, made by UK-based Solarcentury, are attached to the 45x45mm roofing battens, using self-tapping screws. The PV slates overlap each other with a soaker tray between adjacent tiles to form a waterproof surface that doubles as a PV array. The grid-connect inverter, manufactured in Christchurch by Enasolar, is installed in the garage adjacent to the switchboard for easy access. This integrated application resulted in 88 panels covering the entire north-facing side of the roof. This is the first time such an integrated rooftop design—which takes advantage of the ideal roof pitch angle for the PV system—has been used in New Zealand. The system's performance fared better than expected with 5,287 kWh of renewable energy generated in 2013 (with January as the highest producer at 660 kWh and June as the lowest at 269 kWh).

MISSION ZERO HOUSE

———

ANN ARBOR, MI, USA

PROJECT TEAM

OWNER AND DEVELOPER:
Matt and Kelly Grocoff

GENERAL CONTRACTOR:
THRIVE/Matt Grocoff

MECHANICAL ENGINEER:
Haley Mechanical

ELECTRICAL ENGINEER:
Dan's Electric/
Dan Del Loppo

WATER SYSTEM ENGINEER:
BLUElab, University of Michigan

ENERGY CONSULTANT:
MES/Solar Specialists

LIGHTING CONSULTANTS:
Matt Grocoff

WINDOW RESTORATION:
Wood Window Repair

WALL INSULATION:
Farmers Insulation

ATTIC INSULATION:
Arbor Insulation

LANDSCAPE ARCHITECT:
Creating Sustaining Landscapes

SIZE:
2 floors / 1,500 sf*

BUILDING FOOTPRINT:
870 sf

SITE:
8,712 sf

TYPE:
Single Family Home

LIVING TRANSECT:
L3, Village or Campus Zone

WEBSITE:
happyhome.how/tour-my-home

LOCATION:
Ann Arbor, MI, USA

EUI:
19.72 kBtu/sf/year

PV SIZE:
8.1 kW DC**

CLIMATE ZONE:
Cold

ANNUAL ENERGY PRODUCTION:
ACTUAL: 8,939 kWh/yr
NET ENERGY GENERATED:
295 kWh/yr

ANNUAL ENERGY USE:
ACTUAL: 8,676 kWh
SIMULATED/DESIGNED: 8,535 kWh

CONSTRUCTION COST:
$84/sf

CERTIFICATION:
ILFI-certified Net Zero Energy Building

DATE CERTIFIED:
January 2015

*The total conditioned area within the thermal envelope is 2600 sf, including the unvented attic and basement. The total living space is 1500 sf.

**36 225W Sunpower SPR-225-BLK solar panels and 36 individual Enphase microinverters.

63

Located in Ann Arbor, Michigan, **Mission Zero House is a historic preservation of a 1,500 square foot folk-Victorian residence built in 1901, and one of the first homes to receive ILFI Net Zero Energy Building certification. The two-story house features reclaimed materials, restored wood clapboard siding, a full-width front porch, spindle posts and a cut stone foundation. Owners Matt and Kelly Grocoff were looking to restore a home for their family with the goal of achieving net zero energy while encompassing the spirit of community and being ecologically mindful.** The team set out to create a space that met the Secretary of the Interior's Standards for Historic Preservation, and to reimagine the character of a "green" house. The home's solar array required the owners to seek approval from the Ann Arbor Historic District Commission; approval was granted as the solar installation did not affect or damage the building. The visible PV array adds a clear contrast to the traditional house frame. Otherwise blending into the neighborhood, the Mission Zero House adds to the community through its familiar style and boundary-pushing ideals, surrounded by landscaping of native plants and fruit trees.

ENERGY STORY: ACHIEVING NET ZERO AND BEYOND

The goal of the Mission Zero House was to preserve the heritage of the structure, keeping all the existing walls and windows while significantly improving its energy performance. Fortunately, the original home was already well-sited, providing good solar orientation, and the second floor eaves allowed effective shading in the summer. The natural passive stack of the house draws airflow from the basement and attic windows.

The thermal envelope of the structure was improved with insulation, and the energy efficiency measures for solar installation were created through efficient appliances and controls. Perhaps the most interesting aspect of the home is the fact that net zero energy was achievable without an extensive remodel, which has been the standing assumption for NZE homes, particularly in cold climates. The success of Mission Zero House is a testimony to the efficacy of ground source heat pumps, coupled with actively involved owner occupants, demonstrating that NZE is achievable without a heavy thermal envelope.

EUI: MISSION ZERO HOUSE

TOTAL SAVINGS **61.1%**

TOTAL ENERGY USAGE

19.7
EUI

61.1%
SAVINGS FROM BASELINE

50.7
KBTU/SF/YEAR
BASELINE EUI*

*RECS 2009,
Very cold/cold residential
single family category

DESIGN ELEMENTS

Envelope: As a wall insulation retrofit, R-13 dense-pack blown cellulose insulation was blown into the existing walls from the exterior. Limited by the 2"x4" width of the original framing, the walls achieve a value of only R-15, including the plaster walls and exterior wood clapboard.

Basement: The basement foundation walls are made of cut stone block, and are partially below grade. The rim joist cavity was filled with spray foam, and the stone foundation walls were left uninsulated. The basement is partially conditioned and used for laundry and storage.

Attic: The attic was converted from an uninsulated, poorly-ventilated space (vented with gable windows) to a cathedralized, unventilated space using open cell Demilec Sealection 500 spray foam, achieving an R-value of approximately R-29.

Windows: The original windows are single-pane assemblies with wood framing. To improve the energy efficiency of the house, a wood window repair expert restored and weather-stripped the original sashes and hardware. Trapp low-e

FINANCING

Construction contract sum:	$125,800
Price per square foot:	$84*
PV system design and installation (after incentives):	$15,560
Total PV system cost:	$56,000
Total incentives:**	$40,440
Final system cost:	$15,560
Public incentives (state, local, federal):***	$19,000
Private sources:	Personal financing
TOTAL PROJECT COST (excluding land purchase):****	**$125,800**

*$125,800 at 1,500 sf

**$15,000: 30% Federal Tax Credit, $19,440: $2.40 utility company upfront credit , $6,000: Sunpower marketing credit

***The project property was purchased with an FHA 203k Rehab Loan in 2006, with the Solar panels receiving a 30% federal tax credit, $2.40 per installed watt from the utility, and an additional $0.13/kWh for a twenty year generation term. The project received State Historic Preservation Tax Credit Incentives of $19,000, which brought the original hard cost from $125,800 to $106,800.

****The property purchase price was $224,000.

storm windows were added to the exterior. Air changes per hour at 50 Pa (ACH50) were reduced from 15.70 ACH50 before the window restoration to 4.75 ACH50 after restoration and installation of exterior storm windows. EcoSmart insulated cellular shades are used on the interior of the windows.

Heating/cooling/ventilation:
Heating and cooling is provided by a WaterFurnace ground source heat pump. Dealing with four wide ranging seasons can be challenging, so the Mission Zero House features a ventilation system of an Ultimate Air Recouperator 200DX energy recovery ventilator, providing thermal control and ventilation. Hot water is provided by a Rheem HB50RH 50 Gallon Heat pump water heater.

Renewable Energy System size:
Electricity is supplied by an 8.1kW DC photovoltaic system (36 225W Sunpower SPR-225-BLK solar panels plus 36 individual Enphase microinverters). The system produced 8,939kWh during the 12-month documentation performance period.

ZERO COTTAGE

SAN FRANCISCO, CA, USA

PROJECT TEAM

OWNER:
David Baker

ARCHITECT:
David Baker
Architects

CONTRACTOR:
David Baker
Architects;
Contractor of Record
with John Blandin,
Falcon Five

**STRUCTURAL
ENGINEER:**
Double D,
Anthony Alegria

**MECHANICAL
ENGINEER:**
David Baker
Architects

**ELECTRICAL
ENGINEER:**
David Baker
Architects

**PLUMBING
ENGINEER:**
David Baker
Architects

**ENERGY
CONSULTANT:**
Prudence Ferreira,
Integral Impact, Inc.

**INTERIOR
DESIGN:**
David Baker
Architects

**LIGHTING
DESIGN:**
David Baker
Architects

**LANDSCAPE
ARCHITECT:**
Fletcher Studio

Zero Cottage is the result of a deep green study of compact, sustainable urban design. Composed of an 1141 square foot loft residence and woodshop located in a rear yard, Zero Cottage pairs with an existing renovated historic Edwardian style townhouse to complete an active mixed-use complex combining cultural, commercial and residential uses on a typical neighborhood lot. The Zero Cottage started as a passive house project and through design techniques aimed to achieve Net Zero Energy certification through the International Living Future Institute. The requirement that renewable energy be placed on-site appealed to the design vision for the building. The project continues the evolution of an urban site that predates the 1906 earthquake and contributes to the ongoing vitality of the Mission District neighborhood. The Zero Cottage is a very interesting blend of uses, with a small commercial woodshop on the ground floor that manufactures architectural components for the owner's practice, and a compact, highly functional studio loft residence above—all capped by a rooftop deck replete with solar panels and space for gardening and relaxing.With the addition of Zero Cottage, the expanded complex

SIZE:
3 floors / 1,140.97 sf

BUILDING FOOTPRINT:
500 sf

SITE:
3,046.19 sf

TYPE:
Single Family Residence
and Workshop

LIVING TRANSECT:
L5, Urban Center Zone

WEBSITE:
dbarchitect.com/ZeroCottage

LOCATION:
San Francisco, CA, USA

EUI:
8.67 kBtu/sf/year

PV SIZE:
3 kW

OTHER RENEWABLES:
None

CLIMATE ZONE:
Marine

ANNUAL ENERGY USE:
ACTUAL: 3,012 kWh
SIMULATED/DESIGNED: N/A

CONSTRUCTION COST:
$600/sf

CERTIFICATION:
ILFI-certified Net Zero
Energy Building

DATE CERTIFIED:
May 2014

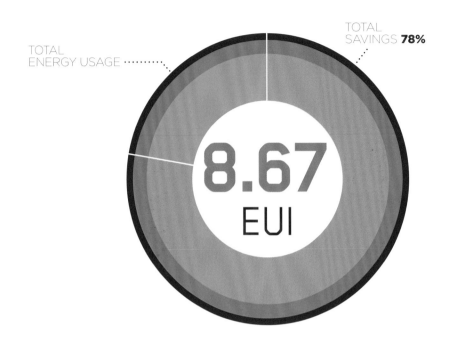

TOTAL
ENERGY USAGE

TOTAL
SAVINGS **78%**

8.67
EUI

78%
SAVINGS FROM
BASELINE

39.7
KBTU/SF/YEAR
BASELINE EUI*

*RECS 2009,
Marine residential
single family category

now houses a changing roster of travelers in the townhouse, as well as StoreFrontLab—a commercial space hosting community-focused cultural events that explore civic space. (Note: The net zero energy performance only applies to the Zero Cottage.)

The Zero Cottage's façade consists of salvaged mirrors and plates of different metals (steel and titanium), creating a unique look and variety for the building. (These elements are readily replaceable and change with weathering.) Planter box "shingles," a playful and functional detail, are relocated throughout the seasons.

Additional exterior cladding is Japanese-style charred wood siding, created from maple flooring salvaged from one of the firm's previous adaptive-reuse projects. The charred wood requires no maintenance, resists fire, rot, and pests, and is expected to perform for more than 80 years. Construction on the building began in March of 2011, and the first occupancy was in December 2012. The relatively mild climate of the Bay Area enables a comfortable temperature nearly year-round and optimal ventilation with fresh outside air.

FINANCING

Soft costs:	N/A
Hard costs:	$688,888
Price per square foot:	$600
Public incentives (state, local, federal):	None
Private sources:	None
TOTAL	**$688,888**

ENERGY STORY: ACHIEVING NET ZERO AND BEYOND

Net zero energy was a baseline goal for the project. Throughout construction, the team continued to refine and improve upon the design to reach net-positive performance. The Passive House standard was selected as the basis for the energy design due to its focus on readily achievable, cost-effective construction methodologies suitable for widespread adoption.

The highly insulated, nearly airtight construction, coupled with a whole-house ventilation system equipped with a heat recovery unit (HRV) aims to reduce heating and cooling loads to a minimum, while maintaining healthy indoor air quality and occupant comfort. By dramatically reducing the heating load through passive design strategies, the design was within reach of serving all remaining energy loads using roof-mounted solar hot water and photovoltaic systems. Fire department roof-access requirements, however, combined with the building's small footprint, severely limited usable space on the roof. The solution, a custom cantilevered solar canopy, turned this obstacle into an opportunity to further improve performance by optimally orienting the double-sided collectors.

DESIGN ELEMENTS

Envelope: The design of the well-insulated, virtually airtight building enclosure addresses two key goals: minimizing thermal bridging, and ensuring that the dew point rests outside of the perm-a-barrier and wall cavity, even during worst-case temperature differentials. Independent Passive House energy modeling initiated after design development revealed points of energy losses due to envelope transmission and ventilation. The team utilized parametric analysis to balance these losses with solar and internal gains. After several rounds of re-testing and refinement, the design achieved the performance targets with thermal resistance of R-29.2 in the walls, R-41.3 at the ceiling, and R-51.2 at the floor. The continuous layer of extruded polystyrene (XPS) surrounding the wall and roof assembly, and expanded polystyrene (EPS) beneath the floor slab was fine tuned to raise the effective resistance of the whole envelope. The walls (R-29.2) are made of gypsum, 2"x6" wood framing and blown-in compressed cellulose insulation with 2-3 inches of outboard XPS insulation. The roof (R-41.3) is similar to the walls, using 2"x12" framing members with the cavity filled with blown-in cellulose insulation, and 6-inches of XPS insulation topped with a green-roof drainage mat, weed barrier and gravel. The floor (R-51.2) assembly between the residential space and workshop uses FSC-Certified Engineered Framing and the cavity is filled with cellulose insulation. The first floor workshop has a 3-inch EPS insulation under concrete slab, taking advantage of EPS's relative low cost to insulate from the ground. With two sides of the lot-line building sitting inches from adjacent structures, achieving the airtight enclosure in the field proved more complex. These corner walls were framed, insulated and sealed as a single L-shaped unit and then lowered into its final position on sill bolts. Blower door tests confirmed that the structure surpassed the Passive House 0.6 ACH (50pa) requirement with an air-change rate of 0.43 (50pa).

Windows: The German manufactured, Sorpetaler TF 78B triple-pane argon windows (U(frame) 0.23; U(glaz) 0.123), with a solar heat gain coefficient (SHGC) of 0.49, while difficult to source, contributed significantly to both energy performance and occupant experience with multiple tilt turn settings.

Heating, cooling, and ventilation: The combination of San Francisco's mild climate and the Zero Cottage's very high performance envelope has resulted in very little need for active heating of the space. A Zehnder ComfoAir 200 heat-recovery ventilator provides heat recovery from shop equipment and electronics and helps balance temperature within the home. The HRV turned out to be a game changer for the space, regulating the already efficient insulation required in the passive house design. The HRV operates at about 300 watts during peak load, and the thermal influence of occupants—each occupant is the equivalent of a 100 watt heater, which makes a difference in compact, well-insulated spaces—also contributes to warming the space. Additionally, there is radiant

ANNUAL ENERGY USE

TYPE + SIZE OF RENEWABLE ENERGY SYSTEM(S) USED:
3 kW Sanyo HIP-195DA3 HIT Double bifacial solar panels

ACTUAL ANNUAL ENERGY USE: 2,897 kWh/yr

ENERGY USE INTENSITY: 8.67 kBtu/ft/yr

ACTUAL ANNUAL ELECTRICITY GENERATED: 5,533 kWh/yr

electric ceiling and floor heating in portions of the building as a backup heating system. In practice this system is used infrequently.

Hot water: A SunEarth "bread box" solar water heater combines thermal collection and storage of water in a single roof-mounted unit. The system can serve as a primary water heater under optimal conditions, and combines with an electric variable-temperature, tankless water heater to meet full hot water needs at other times.

Baseload, Lighting and Appliances: Electric lighting is minimized through the use of a central roof-top light monitor and well-

placed windows. Lighting is supplied exclusively with LED fixtures, most dimmable. Compact, energy-efficient appliances, which further reduce loads, include SubZero undercounter refrigerator and freezer drawers, a Fisher & Paykel single-drawer dishwasher, an LG high-efficiency front-load washer/dryer combo, and a two-burner induction cooktop.

Renewables: A unique feature of the 3kW photovoltaic system is the custom frame fabricated by Henry Defauw, extending beyond the building rooftop acting as a shelter to the staircase below, and as a significant design element, while optimizing panel tilt and placing the panels away from shading. The Sanyo roof-mounted photovoltaics are double-sided, with transparent facing and backing, adding about 5 percent extra efficiency and keeping the panels cooler, enabling them to operate at a higher efficiency level. Aurora DC inverters do not include fans (instead using external heat sinks) and thus are more efficient. Modeling indicated that Zero Cottage's photovoltaic system would generate 3876 kWh/yr of energy, surpassing projected demand by over 860 kWh/yr. Actual generation exceeded these projections in 2013 by 22 percent (over 5,500 kWh/yr). It is possible that the significant increase in production is due to the cantilevered array and the reflectivity of the metal siding below.

COMMERCIAL & OFFICE

BUILDINGS

DAVID & LUCILE PACKARD FOUNDATION HEADQUARTERS

—

LOS ALTOS, CA, USA

PROJECT TEAM

OWNER:
The David and Lucile
Packard Foundation

ARCHITECT:
EHDD

CONTRACTOR:
DPR Construction

**GEOTECHNICAL
ENGINEER:**
Fugro Associates

**CIVIL
ENGINEER:**
Sherwood Design
Engineers

**STRUCTURAL
ENGINEER:**
Tipping Mar
Structural Engineers

**INTERIOR
DESIGN:**
EHDD

**PLUMBING
ENGINEER:**
Integral Group

**MECHANICAL
ENGINEER:**
Integral Group

**ELECTRICAL
ENGINEER:**
Integral Group

**SPECIALTY
CONSULTANTS:**
Ausenco (SCADA
Engineer)

LIGHTING DESIGN:
J S Nolan + Associates
Lighting Design, LLC

**DAYLIGHTING
CONSULTANT:**
Loisos Ubbelohde

**LANDSCAPE
ARCHITECT:**
Joni L. Janecki
& Associates

SUBCONTRACTORS:
SANCO, SYSERCO,
ACCO Engineered
Systems, Western
Allied Mechanical,
Redwood Electrical
Group, Park West

The David and Lucile Packard Foundation Headquarters in Los Altos, California, brings staff, grantees and partners together to solve the world's most intractable problems—working to improve the lives of children, families, and communities, and to restore and protect the planet. For the Packard Foundation's new campus (which began occupancy in July 2012), passive, bioclimatic design strategies (that reflect the organization's core philanthropic mission) serve as the basis of its LEED Platinum building certification and net zero energy performance. The design of the headquarters campus reflects the environmental values the Foundation supports through its work.

SIZE:
2 floors / 50,956 sf

BUILDING FOOTPRINT:
26,335 sf

SITE:
304,920 sf

TYPE:
Office

LIVING TRANSECT:
L4, General Urban Zone

WEBSITE:
packard.org/about-the-foundation/our-green-headquarters

LOCATION:
Los Altos, CA, USA

EUI:
24.38 kBtu/sf/yr

PV SIZE:
Roof-mounted PV panels,
309 MWhr/yr, 285 kW capacity

OTHER RENEWABLES:
Solar hot water

CLIMATE ZONE:
Marine

ANNUAL ENERGY USE:
ACTUAL: 351.30 MWh

DESIGNED/SIMULATED: 277 MWh

ELECTRICITY GENERATED:
418.04 MWh

NET ENERGY USE: -66.73 MWh

CONSTRUCTION COST:
$756/sf

CERTIFICATION:
ILFI-certified Net Zero
Energy Building

DATE CERTIFIED:
September 2013

FINANCING

Hard costs:	$37.2 million
Construction per square foot:	$756

The Packard Foundation's connection to the Los Altos community dates back to its inception in 1964. For decades, as the Foundation's grant making programs expanded locally and around the world, staff and operations had been scattered in buildings throughout the town. This headquarters project enhances proximity and collaboration while renewing the Foundation's commitment to its local community by investing in a downtown project intended to last beyond the 21st century. The project's pioneering focus on sustainability brings its facilities into alignment with the core work of conserving and restoring the earth's natural systems.

EHDD, the sustainably-focused design firm also responsible for the IDeAs Z[2] Design Facility (the first ILFI-certified Net Zero Energy Building; see page 96), designed the Packard headquarters to the highest standards of sustainability. The Foundation's new home, the largest certified net zero energy office building to date, is the cornerstone of its effort to demonstrate how an organization can improve its effectiveness, and the quality of life for its employees, while emitting carbon at the rate needed to keep the global temperature rise below 2°C. (In addition to being a net zero energy project, the facility was designed to have a zero carbon footprint.)

Beyond the goal of energy neutrality, comfort and aesthetics were key elements of the building and property design. (Qualities like thermal comfort and pleasing aesthetics increase levels of employee happiness, and productivity.) Through features like operable windows and blinds and individually dimmable lighting, optimal comfort is achieved by giving control to the users. Through material choices like salvaged eucalyptus, brass, and copper, and design strategies like biophilia, the property is visually stunning. Firmly believing that well-being and style need never be sacrificed for environmentally sustainable design choices, the Packard Foundation Headquarters is as pleasing to the eye and comfortable for the occupants as it is a leading example of net zero energy design.

AWARDS

2012	**STRUCTURES AWARDS, BEST GREEN PROJECT**	San Jose Business Journal
2012	**BEST GREEN PROJECT**	ENR California
2013	**LEED PLATINUM**	US Green Building Council
2013	**NET ZERO ENERGY BUILDING CERTIFICATION INTERNATIONAL LIVING FUTURE INSTITUTE**	Living Building Challenge
2013	**GREEN BUILDING WITH WOOD DESIGN AWARD**	Woodworks
2013	**HONOR AWARD FOR SUSTAINABILITY**	AIA California Council
2013	**COTE TOP TEN AWARD**	American Institute of Architects
2014	**ASHRAE TECHNOLOGY AWARD OF ENGINEERING EXCELLENCE AND FIRST PLACE, NEW COMMERCIAL BUILDINGS**	
2014	**LIVABLE BUILDINGS AWARD**	University of California Berkeley Center for the Built Environment
2015	**POPULAR CHOICE WINNER, ARCHITECTURE + WORKSPACE**	Architizer A+Awards
2015	**MERIT AWARD, EXCELLENCE IN ARCHITECTURE**	AIA San Francisco Design Awards

81

SERVICE
ACCESS
ONLY
DO NOT
ENTER

SITE CONTEXT AND CLIMATE ZONE

The triangular site is made up of 50,000 square feet of building structure, parking, and outdoor space landscaped with native drought-tolerant plants. Based on concept design studies evaluating thermal potential and daylighting, the design is a two-wing building with a south-facing courtyard providing cross-ventilation, maximum daylighting (windows make up about 50 percent of the exterior wall), and a venue for outdoor meetings.

The courtyard features two distinct California landscapes on either side of its seam: woodland and grass. Large deciduous trees act as natural climate control, providing cooling shade in the summer, and sun and light after leaves fall in the winter. The native landscaping—which thrives without fertilizers and pesticides and provides irrigation savings—serves as a valuable habitat for birds, insects, and bees.

Based in drought-prone California, the project's sustainable water practices were well thought out. Rainwater is captured and stored in two 10,000-gallon storage tanks. This supply meets 60 percent of the irrigation needs and 90 percent of the toilet flushing needs of the property. Additionally, waterless urinals, low-flush toilets, and low-flow lavatories, sinks, and showers mean the property maintains a 69 percent lower potable water use than the LEED baseline guidelines for a building. Outside, 90 percent of the landscaping is native, drought-resistant plants maintained via a digitally controlled drip irrigation system.

The design is tuned for the uniquely benign California climate, emphasizing connectivity between indoor and outdoor spaces. The outdoor courtyard functions as the heart and soul of the project. As you move around the building on both floors you are rewarded with a constantly changing view of the courtyard landscape and the building wing beyond. Detailed design studies tested options to ensure a good outdoor microclimate that would be inviting and comfortable year-round, with an optimized length, width and height for both winter warmth and summer cooling.

The green roof garden, visible from the second floor hallways and boardroom, is enlivened by a variety of shallow rooting, low growing succulents planted to create a mosaic similar to the bluffs on the California coast. This garden also provides habitat for birds and insects, reduces peak stormwater flow, and insulates the building interior.

83

ROOF

Type: Wood framing, R-32.5 rigid board insulation, standing seam metal roof

Overall R-value: R-35.7

Solar Reflectance Index: 41

WALLS

Type: 2"x 6" wood frame, 24 inches on center with R-19 insulation between framing and R-4.2 continuous rigid mineral wood insulation with furring strips

Overall R-value: R-18.2

Glazing Percentage: 46.3% window-to-wall ratio

BASEMENT/FOUNDATION

Slab Edge Insulation R-value: 2" expanded polystyrene (EPS) foam, R-8

Basement Wall Insulation R-value: 3" EPS foam, R-12

Under-Slab Insulation R-value: R-8

WINDOWS

Effective U-factor for Assembly: U-0.17

Solar Heat Gain Coefficient (SHGH): 0.25

Visual Transmittance: 0.57

LOCATION

Latitude: 37.38°

Orientation: 328°

Data from High Performing Buildings magazine, Winter 2015 article "Graceful Inspiration" by Peter Rumsey, Eric Soladay, and Ashley Murphree.

ENERGY STORY: ACHIEVING NET ZERO AND BEYOND

Extensive thought and research went into every facet of the planning and design of the Packard Foundation Headquarters. From day one, the design team was focused on replicable and affordable design reflective of its sustainable goals—most specifically, net zero energy performance. To plan the optimal energy efficiencies through integrated design, architects, engineers, and contractors worked together to perform a complete climate and weather analysis, to thoroughly detail the envelope design, and conduct research to estimate energy needs. (Additionally, a comprehensive greenhouse gas assessment was performed, including how employees commute to work, air travel frequencies, etcetera) The team planned for daylighting, shading, solar orientation, and features like continuously insulated wood framed walls and R-7 triple glazed windows for optimal thermal performance (minimizing heating needs).

Energy efficient design strategies reduce energy use of the Foundation building by over 65 percent versus normal institutional buildings. The narrow building wings were designed to be nearly 100 percent daylit, using efficient electric lighting that automatically dims with changing light levels. Similarly, sun shading was built into the design through elements like deep overhangs, balconies, trellises, and trees, and layering of light and shade. Operable windows and blinds, individually dimmable lighting, and office area thermostats provide optimal comfort by giving control to users. Displays alert occupants about when it is appropriate to open and close windows for ventilation. (The building is 100 percent naturally ventilated.) Additionally, the new building design aimed to decrease plug loads by 58 percent largely due to energy savings from Energy Star systems and staff commitment to the energy savings efforts. (Actual energy savings was more than anticipated.)

EUI: DAVID & LUCILE PACKARD FOUNDATION HEADQUARTERS

TOTAL SAVINGS **48.8%**

TOTAL ENERGY USAGE

24.4
EUI

48.8%
SAVINGS FROM BASELINE

47.7
KBTU/SF/YEAR
BASELINE EUI*

*ASHRAE 90.1 – 2007,
Medium office category,
all climates

DESIGN ELEMENTS

Envelope: Considering the project's temperate climate, envelope upgrades allowed mechanical engineers to omit perimeter heating systems. Weather and sun-path analysis optimized the design of solar controls and motorized shades to avoid undesired solar heat gain. Highly insulated walls and roof, and triple element windows maintain temperatures in the space and eliminate almost all need for heating, and most of the need for cooling throughout the year.

Daylighting: The building design, consisting of two long, narrow wings surrounding a center courtyard, reduces energy consumption by maximizing daylighting. Optimally designed to be completely daylit, design elements like building shape, orientation (58 degrees off a true east-west axis), interior shades, and window placement were planned for a 40 percent reduction in the amount of energy typically consumed by artificial lighting in comparable standard commercial buildings. (In the first year of occupancy, actual lighting energy used was 26 percent better than modeled.) Automated systems throughout the building measure natural daylighting levels and automatically dim or brighten artificial light as needed. The integrated design also utilizes both external fixed shading devices and automated shading blinds. Interior shades are user-controlled to combat glare and auto-raise nightly to reset in full daylit mode. Linear skylights and light shelves project natural light farther into the interior space. Dimmable ambient lighting and LED task lighting supplement lighting demands.

Smart energy-saving features: Energy-efficient T-8 fluorescent bulbs, LED task lighting, and workspace occupant sensors that turn lights off and put computers and monitors to sleep when spaces are unoccupied all help reduce building energy use.

Heating, ventilation and air conditioning (HVAC): Indoor air comfort was a top priority in the building's planning. Whenever possible, occupants reduce energy consumption by operating the building in natural ventilation mode with windows and doors open, instead of relying on the conventional HVAC. The building management system features a dashboard that displays real-time data to identify operational efficiencies so that occupants know when to open and close windows and sliding doors in order to optimize natural ventilation and reduce energy consumption.

In cold weather, the building is warmed to a target temperature of 74°F starting three hours before employees arrive at work. Once the workday begins, the heating system typically turns off and the building relies upon heat gain from office equipment and the occupants themselves to maintain a comfortable temperature. The building is heated by a combination of air handlers, and in certain areas, by heated water via chilled beams.

In warm weather, water is cooled at night by a compressor-free cooling tower and stored in two 25,000-gallon underground tanks. During the day, the cool water is pumped into the pipes that run through the chilled beams. Three major air-handling units pull in 100 percent outside air, then filter and dehumidify it. Air flowing across the beams is sufficient to cool the interior spaces.

The chilled water is moved through the system using variable speed pumps and pipes angled at 130 degrees rather than typical 90-degree angles. This is much more efficient than standard practices, allowing for a 75 percent reduction in ductwork and a 75 percent reduction in pump energy.

Energy Monitoring: Individual branch circuit monitoring is employed so that the energy consumption of each load can be pinpointed and pieces of equipment that consume large amounts of power can be easily identified. This energy monitoring is accomplished using electric panel boards specifically designed for the task. Data

OCCUPANCY

In addition to a carbon analysis for the property, a carbon analysis was performed on employee commutes. At the new headquarters facility, the Foundation's Transportation Demand Management Plan eliminated the need for an 8 million dollar parking garage. The property includes 67 parking spaces rather than 160, and incentivizes employees to use alternative modes of transportation. For instance, the Foundation provides a shuttle to and from the local train and bus stations.

With a behavioral approach to energy conservation, certain facilities are centrally located to encourage sustainable practices by the building occupants. For example, print stations are located in common areas rather than individual printers at each workstation. Other design details encouraging energy efficiency include desktop alerts indicating when doors and windows can be opened for natural ventilation.

Serving as a model for sustainable design, and in line with its mission to drive a sustainable future, the Packard Foundation encourages replication of its headquarters. The Foundation's website shares information resources for the project's design that can be replicated for function and energy neutrality in many climates. The public can take a virtual tour of the facility online, or schedule a tour in person.

can be extracted from the panel board's integrated data-logger and used in a variety of ways: scientific research, incorporation into a web-based interface, to monitor and control certain circuits, etcetera. The SquareD PowerLogic BCM panel boards are used for individual circuit monitoring. For loads connected directly to the switchboard—such as the elevator and large mechanical loads—individual meters are used.

Overall building energy monitoring and power generation monitoring is provided in accordance with the California Energy Commission rebate program. All monitoring devices are connected to the building Supervisory Control and Data Acquisition (SCADA) system. Nearly 15,000 monitoring and control points are part of the building automation system.

Renewables: A roof-mounted 285 kW PV array—the building's only energy source—more than offsets the building's electrical load, allowing the building to achieve its net zero energy goal. Based on an energy model, designers anticipated the building would consume 247MWh/yr, so the PV production would allow an offset of 100 percent of the building's energy consumption with a 19 percent safety factor. Energy production calculations were based on the SunPower SPR-318 solar panel, the most efficient panel on the market at the time.

DPR CONSTRUCTION PHOENIX REGIONAL HEADQUARTERS

PHOENIX, ARIZONA, USA

PROJECT TEAM

OWNER:
DPR Construction

ARCHITECT:
SmithGroupJJR

CONTRACTOR:
DPR Construction

CIVIL ENGINEER:
Coe Van Loo

MECHANICAL ENGINEER:
SmithGroupJJR

ELECTRICAL ENGINEER:
SmithGroupJJR

CONSULTING STRUCTURAL ENGINEER:
PK Associates, LLC

PLUMBING ENGINEER:
SmithGroupJJR

INTERIOR DESIGN:
SmithGroupJJR

LIGHTING DESIGN:
SmithGroupJJR

LANDSCAPE ARCHITECT:
SmithGroupJJR

ENERGY MODELING/ SUSTAINABILITY:
DNV KEMA Energy &Sustainability

PV SYSTEM DESIGN:
OMNI Engineering

MEP DESIGN-ASSIST CONTRACTORS
Bel-Aire Mechanical, Inc., Wilson Electric Services Corp

DPR Construction's Phoenix Regional Headquarters creates a space that exemplifies deep sustainability in the hot dry climate, on a site that provides revitalization and adaptive reuse. The office is ILFI Net Zero Energy and LEED®-NC Platinum certified. DPR Construction is a technical general contractor building throughout the United States, including the Southwest and California, and is providing an example of world-class caliber net zero leadership through its offices — in addition to Phoenix, DPR has also built regional headquarters in San Diego and San Francisco that are seeking Net Zero Energy certification. DPR's goal for the Phoenix office was to not only produce more energy on-site than it consumed, but to reimagine the open office environment for over forty employees with passive and active cooling scenarios, including 87 operable windows, a 87-foot long, 13 feet high, zinc clad solar chimney, and a 79 kWh PV solar array on the adjacent parking lot. The project had a tight timeline of just ten months to complete the office, which opened in October 2011 at a total cost of $4,571,280, not including soft costs or the site and existing building. This building is an outstanding example of thoughtful, constructor-driven pragmatism that resulted in a highly cost effective, very compelling building with a nuanced approach to achieving net zero energy usage.

SIZE:
1 floor / 16,533 sf

BUILDING FOOTPRINT:
19,100 sf

SITE:
56,770 sf

TYPE:
Commercial Renovation

LIVING TRANSECT:
L4, General Urban Zone

WEBSITE:
dpr.com/company/offices/phoenix-arizona

LOCATION:
Phoenix, Arizona, USA

89

EUI:
26.7 kBtu/sf/yr

PV SIZE:
78.96 kW, 326 - 235W dc Kyocera modules

OTHER RENEWABLES:
Solar Thermal Array

CLIMATE ZONE:
Hot-Dry

ANNUAL ENERGY USE:
ACTUAL:
129,624 kWh

ELECTRICITY GENERATED:
142,871 kWh

NET ENERGY USE:
-13,255 kWh

CONSTRUCTION COST:
$210.23/sf

CERTIFICATION:
ILFI-certified Net Zero Energy Building

DATE CERTIFIED:
May 2013

CONTEXT AND CLIMATE

The site was first developed in 1964 as a paint store, which later became a windowless adult bookstore. The property was vacant for a period of time before it was purchased by DPR. While much of the space was built as a parking lot, some of that area was converted to host native plants in a green-screened courtyard. The climate of Phoenix is hot and arid, with little rainfall, and temperatures exceeding 110°F through the summer, while dropping to freezing in the cooler months. Sunshine and warmth are abundant but must also be moderated to keep spaces comfortable at the higher ranges. Rather than fight the harsh climate, DPR Construction aimed to embrace the desert challenges and create accommodating functional design.

FINANCING

Soft costs:	$1,095,581
Hard costs:	
Tenant improvements:	$2,216,939
Existing shell interior demo and structural improvements:	$940,483
PV covered parking system and solar water heating:	$404,411
Energy Rebates:	$86,134
Total hard cost per square foot, excluding existing building and land:	$210.23
Public incentives (state, local, federal):	$0.075/kwh Arizona solar production payment. Federal tax credits for PV.
Private sources:	The project was funded by DPR Construction, the owner of the site and occupant of the building.
TOTAL PROJECT COSTS (excluding land and existing building purchase):	**$4,571,280**

ENERGY STORY: ACHIEVING NET ZERO AND BEYOND

Obviously, the primary energy use of the DPR Phoenix building is cooling — Phoenix has the hottest average temperature of any major city in the United States. Rather than simply throwing a large mechanical system at the building, the DPR team took a more subtle approach that recognized different needs of the building during different seasons and time of day. The result is a design that combines passive, simple mechanical, and more complex mechanical systems that stage appropriately. In particular, the building uses both stack effect and evaporative cooling, and fast air movement to regulate internal temperature and comfort. This approach also is more durable — the simpler systems will have a longer useful life, whereas a large heat pump driven system may last for only 15-20 years.

DESIGN ELEMENTS

Envelope: Retaining the original structure, the previous building's concrete, wood and steel frame were left intact, and over 93 percent of the original framing was retained. Window and door openings in the existing shell were created, with west and south facing walls having no windows, and the east- and north facing walls featuring 87 operable windows and, 3 roll-up doors to maximize lighting and minimize solar gain. The concrete exterior walls are insulated with 6 inches of batt

EVAPORATIVE COOLING

The DPR Phoenix building developed a very simple, cost-effective way of cooling the building during shoulder times – when outside temperatures are in their 80s – by creating a simple mechanical system to provide evaporative cooling. Evaporative cooling is a simple physical law – when a liquid turns into a gas, it must pull caloric energy from its surroundings, resulting in cooling. The sense of deep chill when standing next to a waterfall is not just the radiant cooling of the water – as the water falls, a significant amount becomes in gas, and in the process draws significant heat from its surroundings. Evaporative cooling was first discovered by the Egyptians, who had slaves fan air across open jars of water towards appreciative royalty. Later, Leonardo da Vinci created a simple mechanical water wheel which provided evaporative cooling to his patron's wife's boudoir.

The DPR Phoenix building includes a simple, elegant, sitefabricated evaporative cooling system. Four "shower towers", each made of 24 inch corrugated plastic pipe stood on end, contain 2 large, oversize shower heads and a ring with 4 mister heads in each tower, which sprays a fine mist inside the top of the pipe.

As the sprayed liquid water becomes gas, it draws heat from the air. This cooled air falls to the bottom of the tube, which sits atop a standard spec duct, which is open to the inside of the building. The cooled air then spills into the building. The water itself is collected at the base of the tower and continuously recycled.

in the night flush of air, part of the passive cooling strategies in the building. Finally, the building uses its innovative "shower towers" to further cool the building through very simple mechanical means. Active mechanical cooling in the form of high efficiency compressor-based air conditioners do provide peak cooling, but because the building uses very low energy use elements to cool the building in moderately hot periods, the overall cooling load is dramatically reduced.

Hot Water: The site's hot water use is small and takes advantage of the abundant sun and heat in the Arizona desert. The 4500W Rheem solar thermal water heater is a closed loop glycol system that pushes fluid through two collectors on the roof and then to storage in an 85 gallon tank.

and additional gypsum board. The plywood roof features several inches of foam insulation with both metal and wood framing in the building's interior.

Heating/cooling: The space retains cool temperatures during work hours by utilizing a combination of active and passive cooling solutions. The first stage of cooling, used when outside temperatures are in the mid-80s, combines a number of features. Temperature actuated windows open and close depending on outdoor temperatures. During cool Phoenix nights, windows open automatically to capture this air and

store it until daytime. The changing rhythms of the windows are an interesting feature for the occupants because they exemplify a building model that constantly adapts to light, temperature and conditions. An elevated plinth, that runs the length of the building, sitting atop the roof, provides enough vertical separation to allow stack effect ventilation, which draws air up and out through the building. Twelve oversize, large fans strategically placed throughout the office facilitate air movement as a significant and additional aspect of the cooling strategy for the open office. The fans also play a vital role

Daylighting and lighting: Daylight in the sunny southwest is an abundant and free resource that DPR Construction sought to harness for their facility. With ample daylight also comes significant potential solar thermal gain, so moderating that gain was crucial to maintaining a comfortable space. Solatube skylights are placed throughout the building, in addition to the operable windows that facilitate changing light conditions through the day and the seasons. The Solatube skylights use a fresnel lens-based design that refracts light coming into the tube on the roof as well as distributing inside the space. High

DHW **4.3%**

LIGHTING **30.5%**

TOTAL SAVINGS **45.3%**

PLUG LOADS **15.5%**

26.7
EUI

HVAC **50.3%**

45.3%
SAVINGS FROM
BASELINE

47.7
KBTU/SF/YEAR
BASELINE EUI*

93

*ASHRAE 90.1 – 2007,
Medium office category,
all climates

efficiency, artificial LED lighting placed within the building is used as a backup light source for work spaces. In practice, lighting is rarely used, except for task lights — a noted characteristic of most well daylit buildings.

Plug loads: Plug loads are a significant factor in daily building electricity use and several measures were taken to encourage energy conservation. A "vampire shut-off switch" is connected to about 95 percent of the noncritical systems, or "phantom" outlets, which at end-of-day is controlled by the occupants. This "vampire" switch (a large red button) is

popular with the staff, and has resulted in a 37 percent reduction in plug load energy consumption. A Lucid Building Dashboard monitors the energy generation and usage in real time for the building, providing ongoing feedback to the workers about their net zero energy performance.

Renewable Energy: The office has a 78.96 kW-DC photovoltaic array and solar thermal hot water system. The photovoltaic array is connected to the grid via the local utility, Arizona Public Service, and is composed of 366 Kyocera modules. Arizona Public Service provided net metering

services, paying DPR with excess credit for power generated over the site's use. The PV array is mounted on the parking lot canopies, with the first configuration of panels in a cascading array and the second in continuous rows. Both configurations are at a 10 degree tilt and the arrays are positioned on the North and East facing parking lots, clear of shading from the nearby building. DPR made use of the parking canopies to provide shade to the parking lot and to utilize a a large swath of space. This also freed up room for solar tube skylights on the actual building.

Creatively-designed shower towers, using off-the-shelf components, capitalize on the natural phenomena of evaporative cooling.

CONSTRUCTION PROCESS, CONSTRUCTABILITY ISSUES, AND OCCUPANCY

Designing and building a net zero energy building in ten months is not easy. The team found that an owner driven, continuously integrated design and decision-making structure was critical for success. The entire process was managed by a dedicated project manager, with immediate access to the DPR regional director as decision maker. Meeting scheduling proved to be very difficult with large teams, so having a central person driving the narrative thread was critical. During occupancy, a couple of interesting lessons were learned. The automated louver/window program proved to be finicky, consistent with some other projects, but in the end was resolved and works well. The daylighting through the skylights works so well that lighting is rarely used. Overall, the building is well loved by the occupants, which find it to be a very productive place to work.

NET ZERO LEADERSHIP

DPR is walking the talk having achieved ILFI Net Zero Energy Building certification for their Phoenix Regional Headquarters and pursuing it for two additional retrofits with their headquarters in San Diego and San Francisco. This leadership gives DPR unique perspective about what it takes to achieve the ultimate in energy performance.

IDeAs Z² DESIGN FACILITY

SAN JOSE, CA, USA

PROJECT TEAM

OWNER:
Integral Group

ARCHITECT:
EHDD Architecture

CONTRACTOR:
Hillhouse
Construction

**STRUCTURAL
ENGINEER:**
Tipping Mar

**MECHANICAL
ENGINEER:**
Integral Group,
Johnson Controls

**ELECTRICAL
ENGINEER:**
Integral Group

**LIGHTING
DESIGN:**
Opsis Architecture

A pioneering net zero energy building within the United States, and one of the first projects to certify under the International Living Future Institute's Net Zero Energy Building certification program, the IDeAs Z² Design Facility building was commissioned by Integrated Design Associates (or IDeAs), which later merged with Integral Group. IDeAs, an interactive global network of green building design professionals, was looking to take green building to the next level with a net zero energy design facility. Located in San Jose, California, in the relatively mild marine climate of coastal Northern California, the team engaged in adaptive reuse of a minimally daylit bank building from the 1960s, transforming it into an open, bright and comfortable space. The building is naturally ventilated, with monitoring systems alerting occupants they may open windows when the HVAC system is simply pulling in outside air. The largest and main meeting space opens to the outside on all sides. The project offers an outstanding model for deep, net zero retrofitting of the millions of square feet of low density office and warehouse uses found throughout California and similar climates.

SIZE:
2 floors / 7,200 sf

BUILDING FOOTPRINT:
3,250 sf

SITE:
34,000 sf

TYPE:
Renovation - Office Building

LIVING TRANSECT:
L4, General Urban Zone

WEBSITE:
integralgroup.com/gallery/
office/ideas-z-squared-building

LOCATION:
San Jose, CA, USA

EUI:
21.7 kBtu/sf /year

PV SIZE:
30kW AC SunPower A-300
monocrystaline solar cells

OTHER RENEWABLES:
Solar Save, Architectural
PV glass

CLIMATE ZONE:
Marine

ANNUAL ENERGY USE:
44,660 kWh

ANNUAL ENERGY PRODUCTION:
45,841 kWh

CONSTRUCTION COST:
$175/sf

CERTIFICATION:
ILFI-certified Net Zero
Energy Building

DATE CERTIFIED:
April 2012

97

IDeAs Z² demonstrates that even marginal, low grade buildings can be rebuilt into the top tier of performance and function.

DESIGN ELEMENTS

Envelope: The building includes a one-story, 3,100 square foot studio featuring 18-foot ceilings, and a 4,100 square foot, two-story tenant and conference room area. A signature design feature, oversized swinging doors which open onto an internal courtyard, were cut into the existing southern wall. (The original building had five-inch thick concrete tilt-up walls.) The envelope performance was improved by furring the interior walls and adding fiberglass batt insulation, resulting in R-30 in the roof and R-19 in the concrete walls—a small amount, which reflects the region's mild climate. The windows on the south, west, and north, as well as the skylights, are PPG Solarban 70XL Sapphire with a U-value of 0.28 (average), solar heat coefficient of 0.27, and light transmission of 0.63. This product had the highest light-to-solar gain ratio (2.33) available at the time, to minimize the solar heat gain accompanying daylight. On the east edge of the building, Sage electrochromic glass (which was highly innovative at the time) was installed to regulate morning thermal gain and glare. This

IDeAs Z² NET ZERO ENERGY PIONEER

Though the IDeAs building was certified in 2012 (the year the Net Zero Energy Building Certification was created), it was designed in 2005 and occupied in 2007—when net zero energy buildings were just emerging as a concept in North America. At that time, while net zero energy buildings seemed achievable on paper, considerable uncertainty surrounded its aspects: many of the associated technologies, the most cost effective pathways, and whether the buildings would truly perform as modeled. Today, it is momentous that while the concept of net zero energy buildings is slowly becoming better known (though the projects are still few and far between), this thoughtfully executed building is nearing a decade of occupancy. The space provides a comfortable and high performance workspace for the net zero engineers within, inspiring them to build the next generation of Net Zero Energy and Living Buildings.

glass uses a ceramic coating that is electronically dimmable. The visible transmittance of the glass can be varied from 62 percent to 3.5 percent, and solar heat gain coefficient from 0.48 to 0.09. The U-value is 0.28. A photocell low-voltage controller automatically varies the dimming as appropriate. Overall, the glazing system significantly reduces the cooling load of the building.

HVAC: Given its location in the South Bay Area, that is typically warmer than parts of the Bay Area further north, the building is cooling dominated. The building relies on a mix of outside air ventilation and mechanical cooling to maintain comfortable interior temperatures. Because the building design is fairly simple, and is occupied primarily by an extremely knowledgeable user, operable windows provide ventilation and cooling when outside temperatures are appropriate. A ground source heat pump system is provided for peak cooling, as well as heating during the short cold winter

EUI: IDeAs Z² DESIGN FACILITY

TOTAL SAVINGS **44.5%**

21.7 EUI

TOTAL ENERGY USAGE

44.5%
SAVINGS FROM BASELINE

39.1
KBTU/SF/YEAR BASELINE EUI*

*ASHRAE 90.1 – 2007, Small office category, all climates

---

period. The ground source system uses a horizontal pre-warming loop, that is significantly less expensive than a vertical borehole wellfield typically seen on higher density projects. This loop sits under the parking lot. As required, a heat pump heats or cools the water, which is then distributed via a hydronic loop in a topping slab.

Lighting: The addition of new windows and large skylights to the former bank allows the design studio to take advantage of daylighting year-round. Dimmable fluorescent tube T-8s on electronic ballasts (which were cutting edge at the time of construction) provide supplemental lighting, but in practice are rarely used.

User loads: Each workstation is equipped with a power strip that includes unswitched and switched outlets, the latter being connected to an occupancy sensor that shuts off non-critical energy uses when the space is vacant.

Renewables: The building had 2,600 square feet of roof availability, allowing a 30 kW integrated photovoltaic system using SunPower A-300 solar cells. The cells are highly efficient (20-21.5 percent) and are mounted in a highly unusual membrane-integrated system which is flush to the roofing material. A second south-facing PV system, integrated into the building, is part of a laminated glass awning over the main entrance, providing a

FINANCING

PROJECT COSTS: The building remodel budget estimate is $1.26M (about $175 per square foot) excluding site, original building, and soft costs.

signature design feature that allows visitors to experience the solar panels up close—which in 2007 was an exciting and unusual event. Incentives from the California Energy Commission ($2.80 per watt) helped secure the funding for the system, in addition to the federal 30 percent tax credit, which helped reduce the overall cost of the system upwards of 80 percent.

BULLITT CENTER

———

SEATTLE, WA, USA

PROJECT TEAM

OWNER:
Bullitt Foundation

ARCHITECT: The Miller Hull Partnership

DEVELOPER: Point32

GENERAL CONTRACTOR:
Schuchart

CIVIL ENGINEER:
Springline Design

MECHANICAL ENGINEER:
PAE Consulting Engineers

ELECTRICAL ENGINEER:
PAE Consulting Engineers

STRUCTURAL ENGINEER:
DCI Engineers

BUILDING ENVELOPE CONSULTANT:
RDH Building Envelope Consultants

WATER SYSTEM ENGINEER:
2020 Engineering

ENERGY CONSULTANT:
Solar Design Associates, Inc.

LIGHTING CONSULTANT:
Integrated Design Lab | Puget Sound, College of Built Environments, University of Washington

LANDSCAPE ARCHITECT:
Berger Partnership

SIZE:
6 floors / 50,798 sf

SITE:
10,076 sf

TYPE:
Class A Commercial Office Building

LIVING TRANSECT:
L6, Urban Core Zone

WEBSITE:
bullittcenter.org

LOCATION:
Central Area, Seattle, Washington, USA

EUI:
12.3 kBtu/sf/year
2014 DATA

PV SIZE:
244 kW Photovoltaic array, 14,303 sf system, roof mount

OTHER RENEWABLES:
None

CLIMATE ZONE:
Marine

ANNUAL ENERGY USE:
ACTUAL: 137,800 kWh
SIMULATED/DESIGNED: 251,885 kWh

CONSTRUCTION COST:
$359/sf

CERTIFICATION:
Full Living Building Challenge Certified; ILFI-certified Net Zero Energy Building

DATE CERTIFIED:
March 2015

The Bullitt Center in Seattle, Washington features a high functioning, signature design that pushes the limits of energy efficiency, and shapes the future landscape of cities and new possibilities for commercial spaces in the built environment. The Center is home to the Bullitt Foundation, a philanthropic organization with a long legacy of positive change in the Cascadia region, that seeks to create high impact projects and programs focused on environmental concerns. The Foundation has traditionally focused on stewardship and conservation, but over the last decade has evolved to focus on urban ecology. Through the Bullitt Center, the Foundation has created a model of funding strategies around urban development that encourage engagement with the Living Building Challenge. Bullitt Foundation CEO and long-time environmentalist Denis Hayes was integral in guiding the vision of the Bullitt

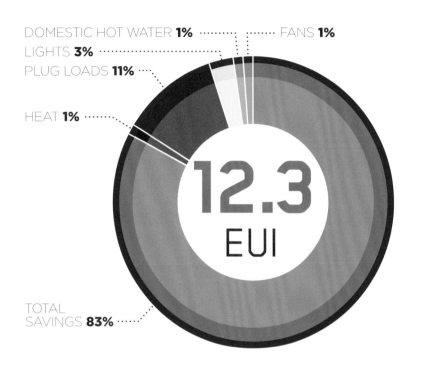

DOMESTIC HOT WATER **1%** .... FANS **1%**
LIGHTS **3%** ....
PLUG LOADS **11%** ....

HEAT **1%** ....

12.3 EUI

TOTAL SAVINGS **83%** ....

83%
SAVINGS FROM BASELINE

47.7
KBTU/SF/YEAR BASELINE EUI*

* ASHRAE 90.1 – 2007,
Medium Office category,
all climates

Center by focusing on strategies that were high impact and measurable.

The decision to build a space was one of great discussion, but when searching for a new Foundation office, current "green buildings" did not live up to the organization's standards. In 2007, during the search, Hayes met Jason F. McLennan (CEO, International Living Future Institute) and was introduced to the Living Building Challenge, which turned out to be the high bar that Hayes was looking for to direct design of the new space. The site was located

for its visibility, close proximity to downtown Seattle, solar exposure and unique modest triangular lot.

The six-story Bullitt Center was the first commercial office space in the world to pursue the Living Building Challenge. While the Bullitt Foundation was highly strategic in its creation of the building, it was essentially acting as a developer—not as a typical institutional, sole occupant— which made the building much more complicated to bring about. The building is a core element of the Foundation's endowment—over 90

percent of the building is speculative, for-lease space (the Foundation only occupies half of one floor), and thus it had to achieve financial returns consistent with the Foundation's other funding and financial needs. Furthermore, unlike most net zero energy buildings with only one user, the Bullitt Center has multiple tenants which represent about half of the building's total energy load, requiring innovative approaches to reducing user loads and ensuring consistent buy-in and coordination across a number of organizations.

The street was vacated adjacent to the Bullitt Center, allowing a direct human connection to the adjacent McGilvra Place Park, a certfield Living Building Infrastructure project.

> "I liked that the Foundation wanted to look at the things that were most urgent and that could be addressed on a time scale that was relevant to us using the resources available. They did not want to jump into anything that would have taken fifty years to determine whether we had succeeded or failed. But at the same time, they recognized that profound changes were needed and that big changes often take time."

DENIS HAYES, BULLITT FOUNDATION

SITE AND CLIMATE CONTEXT

The Bullitt Center is located in a busy urban zone just outside downtown Seattle in the city's First Hill and Central Area neighborhoods. Seattle sits at the heart of Cascadia, a mountainous, green and coastal region on the northern Pacific coast of North America. Seattle is located in the Marine zone with the features of a coastal temperate climate; the Center's design reflects this bioregion. Seattle temperatures range from 20-90 degrees Fahrenheit, with typical winter weather including temperatures in the 40s, clouds, and drizzle. While the average annual rainfall of 38 inches is not unusually high, Seattle is the cloudiest city in the United States (226 days of heavy clouds a year), which is not ideal for solar electric generation and potential passive solar gain. However, Seattle's mild temperatures result in relatively low heating and cooling demand (although more demanding than in cities like San Francisco). The average office building EUI in Seattle operates with primary loads typically around 70 to 95.

FINANCING

Land	$3,380,000
Hard Costs	$23,360,000
Pre-Construction	$450,000
Construction	$18,160,000
Owners Direct	$2,940,000
Sales Tax	$1,810,000
Soft Costs	$5,290,000
Architecture & Engineering	$2,550,000
Permits & Municipal Fees	$320,000
Utility Expenses	$600,000
Testing & Inspection	$140,000
Other*	$1,680,000 *
Sales, Leasing, Legal, Administration, Property Management, Taxes, Insurance, Bonds, Development Services Finance Costs	$470,000
TOTAL	**$32,500,000**

FINANCING

The Bullitt Center's construction cost per square foot came in at $359. Athough this figure is somewhat higher than typical new Class A office costs in the Seattle area, the cost is in line with local premium LEED platinum projects such as the Gates Foundation and Stone 34. In addition, the building's interior shell was highly finished and essentially turnkey, thus requiring minimal tenant improvements and reducing delivered tenant cost. The development team also believed that the knowledge gained in design and permitting through the initial development would result in significant reductions in cost if the building or one similar were replicated. Funding for the project came from the Bullitt Foundation, a loan from US Bank, and a $3.5 million New Market Tax Credit which provides incentive for equity investments within low income neighborhoods. Additional public sector incentives included Federal 1603 program tax credits for the photovoltaic system and heat pumps.

An in-depth study, *Optimizing Urban Ecosystem Services: The Bullitt Center Case Study,* looked at the external benefits of ecosystem services provided by the building to the environment. The study found that the building's energy systems will provide over $13.5 million in carbon reduction benefits over the life of the building—an extraordinary benefit to the community and the planet.

The solar array on the Bullitt Center includes gaps between the panels to allow rainwater and sunlight through. Rainwater is then collected on the primary roof, which sits under the building's solar cap.

ENERGY STORY: ACHIEVING NET ZERO AND BEYOND

The Bullitt Center incorporated a highly sophisticated, iterative design process which evaluated different building forms, window types and solar locations for optimized daylighting, solar electric generation, and wind- and stack-driven passive ventilation. The result is an ultra high performance—yet elegant—building that is one of the most efficient per-square-foot in the world.

In most buildings, the dominant energy demand comes from heating and cooling. As is typical with most net zero buildings, to reduce these loads the building envelope and systems of the Bullitt Center were an area of heavy focus for its design. Broadly speaking, in the Seattle area where passive solar gain is not a source of consistent heating, building layout and orientation is not a critical factor in reducing these loads;

envelope and mechanical systems play a much larger role. However, lighting is usually the next significant user of energy, and daylighting is a primary strategy for reducing lighting energy needs. Daylighting combined with the biophilic need to provide outdoor views were integral to the building's layout.

The Bullitt Center site provided both opportunities and constraints to achieving daylighting within the building. Street right-of-way abuts the site on the north and south, and a legacy park sits to the west. While a four-story apartment complex neighbors the building on the east, ample daylight and views are available on the other three sides of the building. However, the building pro forma and zoning envelope necessitated as much building coverage as possible, and the site itself was 10,076 square feet, which at 100 percent coverage would result in poor daylighting/views in interior locations. To address this, initial schematics included atrium and light well alternatives, but this resulted in less leasable space and impacts to the leasing layout. Greater floor-to-ceiling heights (13.5 feet) were then considered as an alternative; however, this approach required a height variance from the City of Seattle based on their Living Building Challenge demonstration code.

Initial modeling suggested an EUI of 16 kBtu/sf/year for the building, which at six floors would result in more solar demand than could be handled by the full rooftop. Two alternatives were analyzed: one that used a cantilevered roof nearly twenty feet beyond the building footprint for additional solar harvest (this was ultimately chosen), and a second that had a south-facing suspended vertical array. The latter alternative was dropped because of daylighting and view limitation impacts.

DESIGN ELEMENTS

Envelope: The building walls are fiberglass batt insulation in a 2"x6" steel stud cavity with rigid mineral wool outside of the air/water barrier, for a total R value of R-35. The roof insulation provides an R-value of 60. Expanded polystyrene is used under the concrete floors with an R-value of 10. The windows are triple paned and have a U-factor of 0.18. The air and water barriers for the building are combined, and provided through a combination of Prosoco wet flashing over plywood sheathing and windows. The design of the windows allowed wet flash to be applied over the window flange surround, providing a continuous air seal which significantly reduced air leakage.

Heating/Cooling/Ventilation: Heating, cooling, and hot water are provided by a closed loop ground source heat pump. The prewarming field includes 26 four hundred foot deep boreholes located under the building. The building utilizes several heat pumps: one unit each for heating/cooling of two floors, and one pump for domestic hot water, each unit with a single tank. The heating/cooling heat pumps are switched seasonally between heating and cooling modes,

WORLD CLASS, LOCALLY MADE, HIGHLY DURABLE, HIGH-PERFORMANCE WINDOWS

Because a majority of the building façade is glazed, finding the right window system for the Bullitt Center was a top priority. (In a certain way, the building is windows, hung on the structure.) It was necessary to insulate very well, yet allow frequent opening and closing, while maintaining a solid air seal over time. The windows needed to meet the building's impressive 250 year durability specification, and to meet the Living Building Challenge's Appropriate Sourcing Imperative the windows had to be locally manufactured. The optimal windows were found in Germany, manufactured by Schuco International. Featuring triple panes, Schuco's windows pop out of the frame on hinges specifically designed for air circulation. The design was ideal for the project, with a unique seal that met the needs of the air and water envelope of the building. Because the windows did not meet the local sourcing challenge, the Bullitt Foundation and design team helped broker an ideal solution: Local window manufacturer, Goldfinch Brothers, licensed the Schuco International technology and became a local fabricator for the Bullitt Center and any other future projects. These world class windows are now locally available within the Cascadia region. Since supplying the Bullitt Center, Goldfinch has received additional orders for Schuco windows within Cascadia.

providing three advantages: reduced energy use since only heating or cooling are provided at one time; a smaller utility room due to half the number of potential storage tanks (only one tank is provided for either heating or cooling rather than a tank each for heating and cooling); and summer time heating of the ground source field through transfer of waste heat from the heat pump cooling mode. The Colmac heat pumps are manufactured locally in Colville, Washington. Heating and cooling is provided primarily by an in-floor hydronic system in addition to four pipe units in the ventilation supply in the conference rooms.

BIOPHILIA AND LIGHTING AND USER LOADS

A major finding during the Bullitt Center's occupancy was that the building performed better than expected, particularly in the area of lighting and user loads. The reduction of already low energy use assumptions has given rise to significant discussions amongst the energy professionals working in the building as to why this is the case. While in many situations lower user loads are due to more efficient plug-in devices—particularly computers and monitors—there is also a belief that greater connection with nature plays a significant role (and not just in a simple 1:1 reduction in lighting demand).

The biophilic qualities of the Bullitt Center are compelling. All workers have excellent views to the outside. The nature of the daylight gives the interior an entirely different, natural feel than a typical high cubicle/perimeter office workspace. The natural play of light through clouds, trees, the time of day, and seasons all contribute to an environment that is comfortable and restful. Opening windows provides another sensate benefit: the movement of wind and sound from outside.

One very noticeable result is a significant reduction in artificial lighting use, with a lower overall candlepower (daylight + artificial light) than typically assumed necessary for office work. Even on dark evenings, it is not unusual for spaces to be lit only with very low watt LED task lights, ambient twilight and street lighting from outside. In addition, interior kitchen spaces are frequently left unlit, even when relatively dark. It appears that high quality natural light and views to the outside allow for much lower light levels than typical design specifications. It is further suggested that the entire biophilic gestalt of the space reduces the worker's need for artificial alternative comforts like personal heaters and fans.

Solar shading and natural ventilation, that are controlled through a highly sophisticated real-time data driven computer control system, is a key design feature of the Bullitt Center. On an adjacent building, a weather station transmits real-time temperature, wind temperature and speed data to the Bullitt Center building computer. This system measures internal and external conditions and online weather forecasts to regulate the building based on thermostatic controls, opening or closing the windows, as well as raising/lowering external or internal shading to regulate thermal gain. The model is sophisticated enough to open specific windows or shades based on wind direction or sun location. An interactive override system allows tenants to open and close windows independent of computer control (a button is pushed to open the windows, and the system reverts to the most efficient state after 30 minutes). When weather conditions are appropriate during the summer, the building undergoes a night flush of air, with the windows opened at night and closed in the morning to capture and retain cool evening temperatures.

Recognizing that direct outside air is a strategy that works only when outside temperatures are between 60 and 80 degrees Fahrenheit, an additional mechanical, ducted heat recovery ventilation (HRV) system (located on the roof) was also provided (see Glossary for a description of how

HRVs function). The exhaust system runs through the open composting toilet piping, through the composters, then up to the HRV located on the roof. Fresh air supply is provided into conference rooms and CO_2 sensors within the conference rooms further enable ventilation as needed.

Finally, additional cooling is provided by large ceiling fans. Because air movement reduces the apparent temperature for the occupants, these fans are a highly efficient way to increase the cooling set point while providing thermal comfort.

The Irresistible Staircase

A final component of energy savings within the building is the stairway and elevator. The Bullitt Center stands the typical office building design on its head by positioning the stairway in a place of prominence at the entryway, with the elevator located further into the building. Guests are additionally encouraged to use the staircase because it is beautifully encased in glass and cantilevered over the right of way, providing some of the best views out of the building. While the energy impact of reducing use of the elevator is not large, the stairway provides an integrated energy reduction, a

Operable windows allow for a direct connection to the outdoors.

BULLITT CENTER:
YEAR ONE ENERGY USE AND PRODUCTION

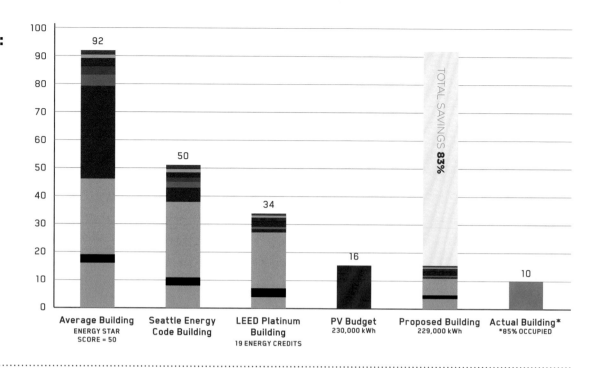

- ■ DOM. HOT WATER
- ■ ELEVATOR
- ■ VENT FANS
- ■ PUMPS & AUX
- ■ SPACE COOLING
- ■ SPACE HEATING
- ■ PLUG LOADS
- ■ IT SERVER
- ■ LIGHTS

symbol for reducing energy loads, and perhaps most importantly, a way for workers to get great exercise while enjoying the view. (Indeed, many occupants take breaks by walking the stairs to clear their head.) As not to compromise the energy performance of the entire building, the design team chose to limit the conditioning of the voluminous vertical space to a level that protects from freezing. Due to the natural ventilation of the staircase its temperature relates closely to the climate of the season.

Renewables
The Bullitt Center's photovoltaic (PV) array produced 244 kW at peak power, and generated 243,671 kW over the course of the performance period. Composed of 575 Sunpower SPR-

425 E19 modules, the array is tilted 5 degrees to the southwest. To provide fire and mechanical access to the primary roof, the panels are mounted on a substantial steel substructure that forms a secondary roof "cap." This substructure, necessary to provide adequate strength for wind and earthquake live loads, substantially increased the cost of the overall array from a base cost of $1.1 million to $1.8 million, including the substructure. Electricity is converted from direct current to alternating current via 20 Sunpower SPR-1140 lf-3-208/240 delta string inverters, mounted underneath the superstructure on the main roof. The SunPower panels were chosen because they met the quality and durability requirements of the Bullitt Center, and were the highest efficiency

panels available, at 19.7 percent, versus the more typical efficiency of 17 percent. The innovative panels achieve this efficiency through a patented back electrical contact that allows the diode to not shade the silicon wafers that generate the electricity. The array is configured with gaps between panels to provide some daylight under the array, to emulate a forest shading patterns, and also to allow rainwater to fall onto the primary roof where it is collected for use within the building. Additionally, the array features a Data Acquisition System, monitoring the performance of the panels, including module temperatures and production. The array is connected to the larger electrical grid, and no energy storage is provided.

The Irresistible Staircase is encased in glass, providing wonderful views of Seattle and the Olympic Mountains – taking the stairway which is typically buried deep within conventional buildings and turning it into an energy saving icon.

CONSTRUCTION, COMMISSIONING, OCCUPANCY, AND LESSONS LEARNED

Construction of the Bullitt Center began in August 2011 and continued through 2012 into 2013. The building was given a certificate of occupancy in April 2013. The relatively long construction time frame took into consideration the significant amount of new concepts and technologies that necessitated additional time to properly construct.

One key challenge was the drilling of the ground source wellfield boreholes which were located under the building and thus had to be drilled prior to installation of the foundation. (The borehole field covers about half the building footprint; the other half is covered by the basement cistern and composting system). Due to the thermal requirements of the system, the boreholes were spaced about fifteen feet apart. At about the 350 foot level, very challenging, soggy soils were experienced that collapsed during drilling, making for very slow progress. Given the nature of the tight urban site, which also included a construction crane, construction sequencing was very challenging. Remarkably, the well driller and construction team were able to place two drill rigs on site at the same time, which allowed the project to remain on schedule.

Another difficulty arose related to energy monitoring at the circuit level. At the beginning of the project, the engineering team created a detailed circuiting/monitoring plan which came to be known as "The Bible." In practice

113

this was very difficult to implement, with significant room for error at both the programming and hardware installation stage. It proved difficult to ensure all tenant improvement electrical subcontractors knew of and used "The Bible." For future projects, the team suggested that individual occupant energy use feedback might be better achieved through individual smart plug meters.

Overall Building Energy Use versus Tenant Loads: Unlike many buildings that have a single user group that can be tasked with the responsibility of achieving net zero energy goals, the Bullitt Center has eight primary tenants and a number of subtenants. The initial energy model determined that about half of the energy use of the building would be "building wide" use under the control of the owner (including base heating and cooling, domestic hot water, common area lighting, and ventilation), and about half of the energy use would be managed by the tenants (tenant space lighting, conference room heating/cooling, plug-in user loads). As a result leases include a provision that lessors are provided an energy use target to meet for their space. The lessor is responsible for the energy bill only if they exceed their energy use budget. As discussed under the design process section above, providing exceptional daylighting for the building played a prominent role in the design process, in large part driven by the fact that

once the heating and cooling loads were reduced significantly, the next highest anticipated load was attributed to artificial lighting. Floor-to-ceiling heights were raised from a typical 10 feet to 13.5 feet, with full height windows placed on the majority of the building perimeter. Combined with these strategies, all tenants in the building use an open floor plan and no cubicle walls, which allows daylight to penetrate deeply into the space as well as affording views to the outside. The result is a quality daylit environment which provides a number of biophilic benefits and reduced lighting loads.

As a supplement to daylighting, artificial lighting is provided by LED and fluorescent fixtures. Within common areas, lights are automated based on occupancy, while leased spaces are left to individual occupant tenant improvements. These tenant lighting options vary all the way from repurposed tube fluorescent box lights installed for construction to modern direct/indirect overhead LED and fluorescent fixtures. In practice, LED task lighting plays a significant role in meeting actual lighting needs beyond daylighting [see inset], with space lighting used infrequently.

Additional user loads are primarily computers and monitors and a diverse array of miscellaneous items such as audio/video electronics, device chargers, and light duty kitchen equipment. A significant finding of occupancy is that technological innovation has led to the rapid lowering of computer-based loads. Most computers in the Bullitt Center are laptops (as opposed to tower units) that consume up to 80 percent less electricity. Additionally, advances in monitor technology has reduced typical loads for a fifteen-inch screen from 75 to 15 watts in the last five years. The net positive result is lower user loads, which contributes significantly to the overall improvement in modeled EUI.

In practice, the Bullitt Center achieved better energy performance than expected. A look at occupancy patterns and realities helps tell the story.

One significant factor is that the office densities are lower than expected and modeled. The density modeled was 175 square feet per person, while in reality, the densities were 200-250 square feet per person, at least during the observation period. This reflects trends in many offices, with the advent of mobile communications and computers, that many employees work remotely in a variety of locations.

Two other significant factors came into play in lower use. The daylighting was so successful that overhead lighting is rarely used, and plug in loads are also lower than expected.

This finding is discussed in the biophilia inset above in more detail.

During the occupancy period, two additional lessons were learned. The night flush ventilation system has proved highly effective in the Bullitt Center, helped by the thermal mass in the concrete floors. During initial occupancy, the night cooling actually activated the heating system, a programming anomaly that was rectified. In addition, the system for manually actuated window opening and closing is very binary, with a single mode which opens all the windows fully in a tenant space for a half hour. In practice, tenants have found that additional settings allowing individual windows to be opened or closed at will would allow for more thermal and sound control.

115

AMERICAN SAMOA EPA OFFICE

UTULEI, AMERICAN SAMOA

PROJECT TEAM

OWNER:
American Samoa
Environmental
Protection Agency

**OWNER'S
REPRESENTATIVE:**
Resilient Design

**CONSULTING
CONTRACTOR:**
RM Construction

**CONSTRUCTION
SUPERVISOR:**
Tim Bodell

CIVIL ENGINEER:
Brian Rippy, Resilient
Design Consulting

**MECHANICAL
ENGINEER:**
AMEL Technologies

**STRUCTURAL
ENGINEER:**
Tinai Gordon & Assoc.

**ELECTRICAL
ENGINEER:**
Victor Chan

PLUMBING ENGINEER:
AMEL Technologies

**GEOTECHNICAL
ENGINEER:**
Tinai Gordon & Assoc.

**LANDSCAPE
ARCHITECT:**
Brian Rippy, Resilient
Design Consulting

SIZE:
2 floors / 7,235 sf

BUILDING FOOTPRINT:
5,000 sf

SITE:
28,266 sf

TYPE:
Office building

LIVING TRANSECT:
L3, Village or Campus Zone

WEBSITE:
epa.as.gov/leed-platinum-
certified-green-building

LOCATION:
Utulei, American Samoa

EUI:
31.9 kBtu/sf/yr

PV SIZE:
56 kW - Blackstar
ASP-390M panels

OTHER RENEWABLES:
None

CLIMATE ZONE:
Tropical

ANNUAL ENERGY USE:
ACTUAL:
67,672 kWh

GENERATED:
69,477 kWh

CONSTRUCTION COST:
$400/sf

CERTIFICATION:
ILFI-certified Net Zero
Energy Building

DATE CERTIFIED:
October 2012

117

The U.S. Territory of American Samoa, located just south of the equator and west of the International Dateline, is a tropical cluster of islands and atolls that boast a unique climate and cultural heritage. The territory government's previous Environmental Protection Agency building was devastated in the September 29, 2009 tsunami, which killed 189 people, mostly in Samoa and American Samoa. As a statement of resiliency and hope, the local authorities sought to rebuild the facility as a net zero energy project. The resulting structure is a testimony to the community's strength and fortitude.

The EPA office is located in the village of Utulei—an area of mixed commercial, office, agricultural, and residential use—and adjacent to a series of government buildings. To reduce the amount of impervious surface, the project includes grass paving, bioretention ponds, ample vegetation and a green roof. With views of Pago Pago harbor and volcanic formations, the design connects the interior and exterior of the building, optimizing social interaction and natural connectivity. The accessible green roof and vegetative space takes advantage of the lush climate amongst a gathering space with full views of the harbor. The design team sought to also reflect the cultural landscape, as well as the

EUI: AS-EPA

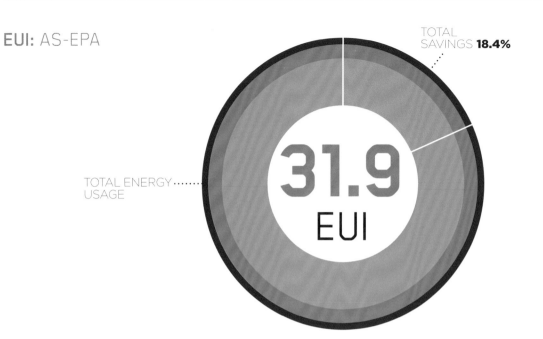

TOTAL SAVINGS **18.4%**

31.9
EUI

TOTAL ENERGY USAGE

18.4%
SAVINGS FROM
BASELINE

39.1
KBTU/SF/YEAR
BASELINE EUI*

*ASHRAE 90.1 – 2007,
Small Office category,
all climates

regional environment, through traditional Samoan motifs adorning high wood-lined ceilings, lanais, and exposed columns. Occupant health and well-being was a key intent of the building design, meant to enhance work performance.

Educational opportunities are available through a kiosk in the building, training sessions, and regular public tours. Local contractors and professional consultants hired by the AS-EPA completed the construction and they have introduced the ILFI-Net Zero Energy Certification and LEED rating system into the region.

ENERGY STORY: ACHIEVING NET ZERO AND BEYOND

The AS-EPA Net Zero Building sought numerous methods for energy conservation. The staff green team has implemented multiple approaches including in-house occupant energy conservation and efficiency teaching sessions, a reward system for conservation measures, and the optimal configuring of technology systems for the building load. These operational measures combined with good building design have reduced the energy demand by 50 percent (which translates

to a savings of $25,000 annually). The PV array was an important first measure, allowing for a significant reduction in the size of the system.

The grid connected photovoltaic system is a 56 kW DC PV array composed of Blackstar ASP-390M panels separated into three arrays of 48 modules above the carport and six arrays of 96 modules on the office roof with SMA-SB7000 inverters. Using underground conduits to connect the two arrays, the systems are monitored

with eGuag software for real-time performance. The employees and the public can access this real-time data linked on the American Samoa EPA website, connecting users and onlookers with energy use and seasonal trends of the building.

Initially, part of the system was not online and in the first months of the building's occupancy it was just short of the intended net zero goal. With the additional array and efficiency measures, the AS-EPA building now operates as a net positive site, producing more electricity than it consumes.

FINANCING

Soft costs:	$300,000
Hard costs:	$2,900,000
Cost per square foot:	$400
Public incentives (state, local, federal):	Funding came from AS-EPA, US-EPA, Territorial Energy Office, the American Samoa Department of Commerce, and National Oceanic and Atmospheric Administration (NOAA).
Private incentives:	None
TOTAL PROJECT COST:	**$3,200,000** (excluding land purchase)

The building's green roof helps to reduce solar heat gain and lowers the operating temperature of the solar panels, thereby improving panel efficiency.

DESIGN ELEMENTS

The AS-EPA project was initially designed to lead the region in green building, seeking LEED certification with a budget of $1.5M. When the design process was completed and construction began, other sustainable design professionals and additional funding sources (bringing the total to over $3.2M) were identified. These resources enabled the addition of a green roof, envelope shading, additional daylighting, and a PV array—all of which made the net zero goal possible. The EPA was also able to implement more efficiency measures and occupant training.

Site orientation: The site's orientation provided space to lengthen the building along an east-west axis, providing passive solar advantages such as cooling, solar shading and positioning for natural ventilation. The transformation of a parking area to vegetated space also reduced the heat island effects of nearby gravel and concrete surfaces.

Envelope: The AS-EPA building is insulated with a concrete envelope of 6 inches under the rooftop deck and garden. These areas are insulated with rigid cellular polyisocyanurate thermal boards about 2 inches thick in the roof. The office design includes R-15 walls and R-30 roof to prevent a thermal bridge from forming. The building's front-facing windows feature a double pane filled with argon, a common feature of well constructed buildings in the tropical climate. The building also houses multiple operable, hurricane fortified windows positioned in aluminum frames with a U-Value of 0.48 glazing. Solar shading is another prominent feature of the building, used to reduce interior temperature gain. The PV and roof vegetation also assist in reducing solar thermal gain. Because of the effective envelope, maintaining a comfortable indoor climate (against the warm average temperature of 88 degrees F) has been successful.

The previous EPA building was demolished by the Samoa tsunami of September 29, 2009. This net zero building was built, in part, as a statement of resiliency.

Daylighting: The effective use of daylight was a central goal of the project and the additional funding allowed for an increase in measures such as more windows and newer south elevation window glazing. The interior lighting is connected with sensors and the long east-west positioning of the building allows for outdoor ventilation and passive comfort. The lighting primarily consists of LED and T-5 fluorescent fixtures that along with the sensors can control features such as dimming, scheduling, and reduction of electricity load.

HVAC: In the hot-humid tropical climate, natural ventilation in the exterior living spaces (such as the lanai) is key. For much of the active parts of the interior, the AS-EPA Net Zero Building uses a variable refrigerant volume (VRV) split HVAC system for air conditioning (cooling) and ventilation. The server room has a separate, smaller, air-cooled condensing unit, providing 24-hour cooling on the first floor to maintain the proper equipment temperature. The toilets, showers, electrical closet and storage rooms are not connected to the main VRV system. The AS-EPA building's CFC refrigerant-free HVAC system is centrally controlled on the first floor to allow scheduling with individual thermostat controls available in the building's different thermal spaces.

Renewables: On-site renewable energy generation consists of a 56 kW photovoltaic system mounted on the office building roof (38 kW) and the adjacent carport (19kW). The panel modules are Blackstar ASP-390M (390w-DC each) and the string inverters are SMA-SB7000 (7000w). P.V. generation is monitored via an eGuage energy monitoring system.

INSTITUTIONAL

BUILDINGS

123

TYSON
LIVING LEARNING
CENTER

EUREKA, MO, USA

PROJECT TEAM

OWNER:
Washington University

ARCHITECT:
Hellmuth + Bicknese
Architects

CONTRACTOR:
Bingman Construction
Company

**STRUCTURAL
ENGINEER:**
ASDG, LLC

CIVIL ENGINEER:
Williams Creek
Consulting

**GEOTECHNICAL
CONSULTANT:**
Grimes Consulting

**LANDSCAPE
ARCHITECT:**
Lewisites

**SPECIALTY
CONSULTANTS:**
Clivis Multrum;
Missouri Solar, LLC

**MECHANICAL,
ENGINEERING
AND PLUMBING:**
Solutions AEC

One of the first two fully certified Living Buildings, the Tyson Living Learning Center at Washington University's Tyson Research Center overlooks nearly 2,000 acres of wilderness near the St. Louis metropolitan area. In 2010, the facility obtained Living Building status under the 1.3 version of the Standard, providing a dedicated environment-related teaching and research space surrounded by a sprawling nature preserve. Situated in a mixed-humid region in the heartland of the United States, the Tyson Living Learning Center is sited on previously developed land, avoiding disturbance to the surrounding landscape.

SIZE:
1 floor / 2,968 sf

BUILDING FOOTPRINT:
2,728 sf

SITE:
24,751 sf

TYPE:
Institutional Building

LIVING TRANSECT:
L1, Natural Habitat Preserve
(Greenfield sites)

WEBSITE:
tyson.wustl.edu/llc

LOCATION:
Eureka, MO, USA

EUI:
24.5 kBtu/sf/year

PV SIZE:
23.1 kW

**TYPE OF RENEWABLE ENERGY
SYSTEMS USED:**
Evergreen Solar Roof &
pole-mounted photovoltaic

OTHER RENEWABLES:
N/A

CLIMATE ZONE:
Mixed-Humid / Heartland

ANNUAL ENERGY USE:
ACTUAL: 21,291 kWh

**ANNUAL ELECTRICITY
GENERATED:**
22,985 kWh

CONSTRUCTION COST:
$523/sf

CERTIFICATION:
Full Living Building Challenge
Certified; ILFI-Certified
Net Zero Energy Building

DATE CERTIFIED:
October 2010

125

ENERGY STORY:
ACHIEVING NET ZERO AND BEYOND

The Tyson Living Learning Center approached the challenge of achieving net zero energy with a whole building focus closely adhering to the principles of minimizing energy demand while maximizing building efficiency. On-site renewable energy production was chosen to generate the necessary power for the classroom. (Wind power was ruled out because the project is located in a valley and the wind turbine would have to be located on higher ground, compromising undeveloped land in a low capacity region for turbines.) The building's south facing slope roof proved to be the most efficient mount area for the PV solar panel array, reducing the need for additional modules. The solar modules are connected with two Fronie inverters feeding the grid with 23.1 kW at peak power production, linking to the grid for storage and balancing the project as net positive for renewable energy. A strategy of engaging building occupants through energy checklists keeps the current electricity use efficient and the participants aware of their energy actions. Net zero energy buildings are a newer concept in the Midwest and are proving to be highly viable. Leading by example, a regional renewable energy provider was chosen to help work with the project's electrical engineer to find the most efficient and cost-effective system for the Center. Reaching an agreement with the local utility was easy; however, the project encountered challenges with the county regulators who

EUI: TYSON LIVING LEARNING CENTER

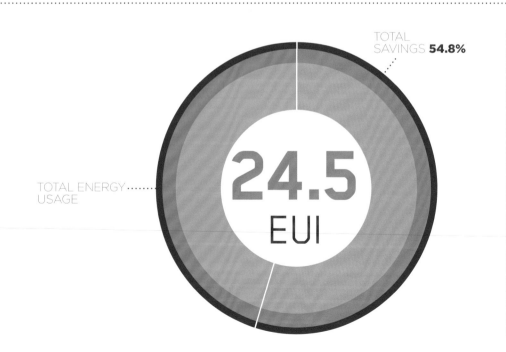

TOTAL SAVINGS **54.8%**

TOTAL ENERGY USAGE

24.5 EUI

54.8%
SAVINGS FROM BASELINE

54.2
KBTU/SF/YEAR
BASELINE EUI*

*ASHRAE 90.1 – 2007,
Secondary school category,
all climates

required a licensed electrical engineer to do the install—which created a conflict between the engineer and the solar installer. A compromise was reached by having the solar supplier assist the contractor in design and installation. This unforeseen delay and extra work resulted in higher costs and is something to consider for future projects that will benefit from a thorough understanding of local requirements pertaining to the installation of photovoltaics and other renewable electricity technologies.

FINANCING

Soft costs:	$169,513
Hard costs:	$1,427,764
Price per square foot:	$523*
Public incentives (state, local, federal):	Austin Energy's Value of Solar Tariff
Private sources:	None
TOTAL PROJECT COST (excluding land purchase):	**$1,597,277**

*$1,427,764 / 2,728 ft = $523 (exclusive of land)

DESIGN ELEMENTS

Envelope & Heating/Cooling: Perhaps the most formidable challenge of the Living Building Challenge is to produce a building that performs as a Net Zero Energy Building. The rooftop PV array being just one part of the energy equation, the building design had to be considered before modeling for energy generation. The design team members approached energy on two basic fronts. First, they limited the amount of required energy the building would consume, and second, they included on-site renewable energy generation capable of handling the energy needs of the building. The most detailed aspect of this two-pronged approach was the task of limiting the building's required energy consumption. These strategies were implemented in conjunction with proper owner training to ensure systems were operating efficiently.

The Tyson Living Learning Center includes a myriad of energy efficiency features. The building's roof and wall insulation has a U-value of 0.03. Domestic water is heated with tankless point-of-use water heaters. Designed to optimize fresh air building ventilation, the windows are operable and the demand-controlled ventilation system features a variable volume outdoor air unit with energy recovery for thermal regulations. The building also utilizes a high efficiency variable refrigerant HVAC system. This system features several different units working in individual areas and is anticipated to reduce the HVAC load by approximately 40 percent over a standard split system. An air-cooled condensing unit, that benefits from heat transfer, keeps the space cool and replaces equipment that would otherwise use harmful CFCs and HCFCs. An Energy Recovery Ventilator (ERV) draws in fresh air and expels exhaust air through multiple fan channels, taking advantage of energy transfer from the exhaust to the outdoors, therefore reducing the need to condition the incoming air. The higher occupancy areas of the Center have sensors that monitor CO_2 levels to increase the ventilation of outside air. Variable refrigerant volume units operate with on-demand temperature regulation including a condenser and multiple evaporators designed to meet the needs of the building. An electric unit heater serves to warm the space when necessary.

Windows and lighting: Each space in the Tyson Living Learning Center has ample daylighting and offers views to the outdoors, with a minimum of one window in all spaces. Natural ventilation is encouraged to connect the indoor and outdoor spaces through light and fresh air circulation

when the weather is suitable. Indoor air quality is further enhanced by low or zero VOC finishes, zero VOC paints, walk-mats in high traffic areas for reducing particulates, and a green cleaning program. The building features high efficiency glazing on the windows with U-values of 0.25, SHCG=0.39. The structure is oriented to limit summertime solar gain through windows while being beneficial to the PV installation on the roof. Exterior overhangs and awnings effectively shade the windows. Occupancy sensors are located in the building to minimize the use of additional lighting (highly efficient fluorescent). The photocell sensors also respond to dimming during daylight hours to further reduce energy output. The restrooms, with operable windows and a solar tubular skylight providing natural light, feature composting toilets utilizing negative pressure to carry air down the channels while pulling fresh air into the space.

Renewables: Ninety-six 195 Watt Evergreen photovoltaic modules have been installed on the sloped metal roof and free-standing poles. Output from the arrays is converted from DC to AC energy by two Fronius inverters. This system feeds the building and the utility grid with approximately 17 kW of peak power production.

The Tyson Living Learning Center includes a ground-mounted solar array, allowing visitors to experience the technology up close.

SMITH COLLEGE'S BECHTEL ENVIRONMENTAL CLASSROOM

WHATELY, MA, USA

PROJECT TEAM

OWNER: Smith College

ARCHITECT: Coldham & Hartman Architects

SURVEYOR:
Berkshire Design Group

GEOTECHNICAL ENGINEER:
O'Reilly, Talbot & Okun

CIVIL ENGINEER:
Berkshire Design Group

LANDSCAPE ARCHITECT:
Dodson Associates

STRUCTURAL ENGINEER:
Ryan S. Hellwig, PE

SYSTEMS DESIGN CONSULTANT:
South Mountain Company, Marc Rosenbaum

INTERIOR DESIGN:
Lorin Starr Interiors

MECHANICAL & PLUMBING ENGINEER:
Kohler & Lewis

ELECTRICAL ENGINEER:
Sager Associates

LIGHTING DESIGN:
Coldham & Hartman Architects

CONTRACTOR:
Scapes Builders

RENEWABLE ENERGY CONTRACTOR:
PV Squared

MECHANICAL CONTRACTOR:
Dobbert Companies

ELECTRICAL:
Martin Electric

Smith College's Bechtel Environmental Classroom—the Ada & Archibald MacLeish Field Station—is one of the most sustainable buildings for higher education in the United States, and was fully certified under the Living Building Challenge in January 2014. Notably, the original RFP called for a "World-class building as LEED Platinum"; however, Coldham and Hartman proposed the project aspire to meet the Living Building Challenge, as the firm's interpretation of "World-class" meant that there was only a handful of projects that had achieved the requirements of the Challenge. Financed by the S.D. Bechtel, Jr. Foundation, the Bechtel Environmental Classroom

---

SIZE:
1 floor / 2,300 sf

SITE:
69,000 sf

TYPE:
Institutional building

LIVING TRANSECT:
L1, Natural Habitat Preserve (Greenfield sites)

WEBSITE:
smith.edu/ceeds/ macleish_bechtel.php

LOCATION:
Whately, MA, USA

EUI:
13.19 kBtu/sf/year

PV SIZE:
9.6 kW

OTHER RENEWABLES:
None

CLIMATE ZONE:
Cold

ANNUAL ENERGY USE:
ACTUAL:
8,892 kWh

SIMULATED/DESIGNED:
9,730 kWh

CONSTRUCTION COST:
$599/sf

CERTIFICATION:
Full Living Building Challenge Certified; ILFI-Certified Net Zero Energy Building

DATE CERTIFIED:
January 2014

131

is a fully fledged educational space, which grew beyond initial plans as a part-time use pavillion. The building takes the next step in Smith College's commitment to sustainability by introducing the Living Building Challenge in a way that creates a platform for student learning. The total project cost amounted to $1,787,000, with a hard cost of $1,377,815 and $54,375 allocated to the solar array. Located on a 69,000 square foot site next to a mixed historic agricultural area, wetland preserve and restored forest in Western Massachusetts, the building is meant to embrace the forested and pastoral setting, featuring natural wood on the interior and biophilic elements on the exterior. Students experience the site as a gateway to studying the surrounding landscape.

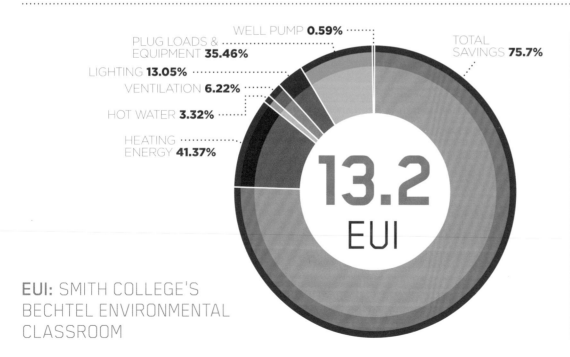

PLUG LOADS & EQUIPMENT **35.46%**

WELL PUMP **0.59%**

LIGHTING **13.05%**

VENTILATION **6.22%**

HOT WATER **3.32%**

HEATING ENERGY **41.37%**

TOTAL SAVINGS **75.7%**

13.2 EUI

EUI: SMITH COLLEGE'S BECHTEL ENVIRONMENTAL CLASSROOM

75.7%
SAVINGS FROM BASELINE

54.2
KBTU/SF/YEAR BASELINE EUI*

*ASHRAE 90.1 – 2007, Secondary school category, all climates

ENERGY STORY:
ACHIEVING NET ZERO AND BEYOND

During the project certification period, the building produced 88 percent more energy than it used, resulting in a significant net positive energy situation. The building utilizes a classic combination of a high-performance envelope, heat pump-based heating and cooling, and on-site solar electric panels to achieve a remarkable level of energy performance. The building is designed as a teaching tool, where occupants interact with it through manual lighting switches (and reminders to create thoughtful usage habits) rather than through automated sensors. All lighting is operated "manual on" or "manual off" with the exception of the basement.

Like many net zero energy buildings, the Smith Bechtel classroom has deep window sills as a result of increased insulation, providing an attractive, substantial feel to the building.

DESIGN ELEMENTS

Envelope: The ceiling is insulated with a thickness of 18 inches of cellulose and the walls with 11.5 inches of cellulose. The R-value of cellulose is 3.5 per inch, resulting in ceiling and roof values of R-63 and R-40, respectively. An air barrier comprised of taped sheathing on the walls and roof combined with Todol Pur Fill low expansion foam spray sealant around the window frames was carefully designed to minimize air leakage. Triple pane, argon-filled windows, provide a U-value of 0.12 for the fixed windows and 0.16 for the operable windows, with a SHGC of 0.46. High south-facing windows support temperature regulation and ventilation in addition to facilitating some daylight, while low-set windows on three sides of the building provide ample daylight, minimizing the need for artificial daytime lighting. The building's position and surrounding trees shade it from the west, minimizing thermal gain.

Heating/cooling: Primary heating is provided by two mini-split ductless heat pumps (Mitsubishi FE 12 and 18). Two Zehnder ComfoAir 550 energy recovery ventilators (87 percent efficient for heat and 89 percent for cooling) recover heat from the exhaust air. Both units are easily accessible—one unit located in the attic and the other in the basement of the building. The ERV units supply 100 percent outside air while preheating that outdoor air, making the space more efficient and reducing thermal demand. The components of the heat pumps are strategically located in the attic and basement of the building acting to maintain a temperature of 60-65 degrees F. This temperature range is ideal for the composting toilets, maintained by ventilation from the ground floor, thermal waste from the water heater and insulated walls and floor. Also, the PV inverters contribute a small amount of heat to the space.

In warmer months, operable windows provide fresh air from the rural setting. The building is very well shaded, but in the case of mechanical cooling, the air-sourced heat pump system can deliver it as an integral part of its operation. The energy recovery ventilation system contributes additional ventilation, while a second exhaust fan, connected to the composting toilet, pulls the exhaust air through the toilet pipes and down to the composting containers. The ventilation system is connected to a CO_2 monitor that activates the system when CO_2 levels are too high.

Additional building features: An on-demand electric resistance hot water heater provides domestic hot water, and its waste heat helps to boost basement temperatures. The classroom uses high recessed LED downlighting and the multi-use space houses cove linear fluorescent lighting, as well as LEDs, using only 840 watts through 22 fixtures, which provide 40 lumens per square foot. Energy and water use are monitored by an Alerton schematic monitoring system. Visual indicators were created as meters for learning and interaction based on categories such as water use, hot water consumption, and electricity generated from the solar panels.

Renewables: Two pole-mounted arrays—each consisting of a total of 15 SunPower SPR-320E-WHT-D modules—generate 9.6 kW which translate to the regional power grid through a single SunPower SPR-1000f-1UNI inverter. Located just to the north of the building, the panels reside on elevated mounts to avoid shade from nearby trees sheltering the building and wetland, and keeping them away from the roof. The project did not receive a financial incentive from the State of Massachusetts, instead electing to keep the Solar Renewable Energy Certificates (SREC) for the claim to environmental attributes of the renewable energy array (see Glossary for details). The array is design-ready for future expansion and the school has obtained the correct permits for additional mounts and connections if demand at the site increases.

FINANCING

Construction contract sum:	$1,377,815
Price per square foot:*	$599
F&E:	$45,000
PV system design and installation:	$54,375
Public incentives (state, local, federal):**	Not Available
Private sources:	Grant from Bechtel Foundation***
TOTAL PROJECT COST (excluding land purchase):	**$1,787,000**

*$1,377,815 / 2300 square feet
**The MA incentive for solar was not taken as the project wanted to keep the renewable energy attributes of the on-site solar array.
*** Amount not disclosed

HAWAII
PREPARATORY
ACADEMY
ENERGY LAB

———

KAMUELA, HI, USA

PROJECT TEAM

OWNER:
Hawaii Preparatory
Academy

ARCHITECT:
Flansburgh
Architects

INTERIOR DESIGN:
Lab 2.0.

CONTRACTOR:
Quality Builders Inc.

CIVIL ENGINEER:
Belt Collins Hawaii

**MECHANICAL
ENGINEER:**
Hakalau Engineering

**STRUCTURAL
ENGINEER:**
Walter Vorfield
& Associates

**ELECTRICAL
ENGINEER:**
Wallace T. Oki, PE Inc.

**GEOTECHNICAL
ENGINEER:**
Geolabs

PLUMBING:
Hakalau Engineering

**LANDSCAPE
ARCHITECT:**
Ken & RMG

**SPECIALTY
CONSULTANTS:**
Buro Happold,
Sustainability and
LEED Quality Builders
Inc, Pa`ahana
Enterprises LLC,
Project Manager

Conceived as a high school science building dedicated to the study of
alternative energy, the Energy Lab at Hawaii Preparatory Academy
functions as a net zero energy, fully sustainable building. The project's
fundamental goal is that of educating the next generation of students in the
understanding of environmentally conscious, sustainable living systems.

The building's donor, the founder of a German alternative energy corporation,
believed that only through generational education will society truly achieve
improved patterns of sustainability; that conserving resources can help to
eliminate conflict and change the patterns of human behavior. Based on his
ideals he challenged the design team to develop a green science building,
insisting that it be powered principally by alternative means. The design team
and Hawaii Prep's Science Department Head furthered these goals, expanding
the mission to include a great number of building systems that employ sun, water
and wind. The project targeted, and subsequently achieved, LEED Platinum
and Living Building Challenge certifications. Completed in January 2010, the
Energy Lab now thrives as a living laboratory, furthering its educational goals as
a functioning example of sustainability. The building has a very low Energy Use

---

SIZE:
1 floor / 5,902 sf

BUILDING FOOTPRINT:
11,535 sf

SITE:
95,832 sf

TYPE:
School/Educational

LIVING TRANSECT:
L3, Village or Campus Zone

WEBSITE:
hpa.edu/academics/energy-lab

LOCATION:
Kamuela, HI, USA

EUI:
11 kBtu/sf/yr

PV SIZE:
26.13 kW (3 separate arrays)

OTHER RENEWABLES:
None

CLIMATE ZONE:
Temperate. Dry

ANNUAL ENERGY USE:
ACTUAL:
19,090 kWh

SIMULATED/DESIGNED:
37,461 kWh

ELECTRICITY GENERATED:
38,994 kWh

CONSTRUCTION COST:
$400/sf

CERTIFICATION:
Full Living Building Challenge
Certified; ILFI-certified
Net Zero Energy Building

DATE CERTIFIED:
April 2011

Intensity of 11 kBtu/sf (significantly less than the campus average of 52 kBtu/sf), providing an aspirational model of energy performance for the school and the entire state of Hawaii. The Energy Lab was developed in response to the high school-level science curriculum it houses. From small project rooms to a large research center and laboratory, spaces were designed to encourage student discovery, exploration and experimentation. Inspired by the designs of tropical modernist and environmental mid-and late- 20th century Hawaiian architect Vladimir Ossipoff, the building's configuration facilitates scientific study both indoors and outdoors, linking interior spaces with the surrounding landscape. Students are surrounded by the systems that they study, and they are constantly being reminded of their functions. Hawaii Prep's Energy Lab offers a continuous, sustainable "teaching moment." Student engagement in the lab has evolved over time, resulting in an array of alternative energy education work. Field work on sugarcane and Jatropha-based biofuels has been established, as well as the growing of traditional native crops such as taro and sweet potato.

Solar panels are easily visible on the Hawai'i Preparatory Science Lab, helping the building to be an integral part of the school's energy curriculum

SITE CONTEXT AND DESIGN PROCESS

The Energy Lab is located in a very unique microclimate, sitting at about 2,500 feet on the north tip of the Big Island of Hawaii. While the state of Hawaii may conjure notions of a consistent hot humid climate—and is entirely designated as such by the U.S. Department of Energy—in reality, it has one of the most diverse set of microclimates in the world (there are two 14,000+ foot peaks on this roughly 60-mile-by-60-mile island). On the Big Island alone, there are eight distinct climate zones, including monsoon, desert, tundra, and nearly everything between. The school itself is situated in a temperate dry-warm climate, below the Kohala range which sits north of the school. A consistent north wind blows, coming off the Pacific and up and over the Kohala Range to the school.

FINANCING

Soft costs:	$1,314,569
Hard costs:	$6,991,630
Price per square foot:	$606
PV system cost:	$200,000
Public incentives (state, local, federal):	None
Private sources:	The majority of the project funding came from private donations, including $2 million from Hawaii Preparatory Academy funds and $6.334 million from a single donor.
TOTAL PROJECT COST (excluding land purchase):	**$8,306,199**

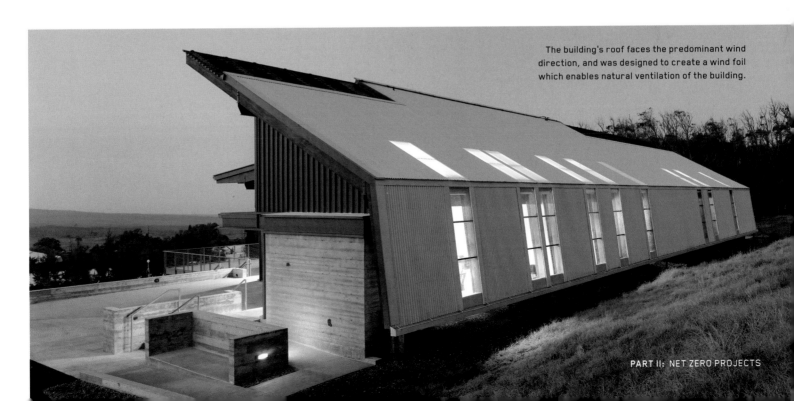

The building's roof faces the predominant wind direction, and was designed to create a wind foil which enables natural ventilation of the building.

PART II: NET ZERO PROJECTS

EUI: HAWAII PREPARATORY ACADEMY ENERGY LAB

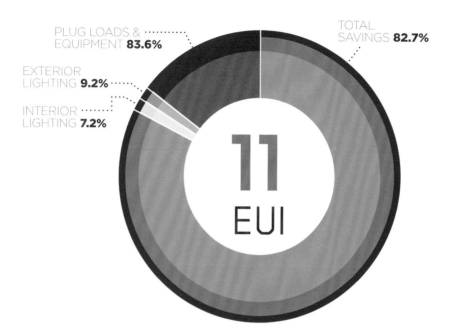

PLUG LOADS & EQUIPMENT **83.6%**

EXTERIOR LIGHTING **9.2%**

INTERIOR LIGHTING **7.2%**

TOTAL SAVINGS **82.7%**

11 EUI

82.7%
SAVINGS FROM BASELINE

63.4
KBTU/SF/YEAR BASELINE EUI*

*ASHRAE 90.1 – 2007, Primary school category, all climates

The Hawaii Preparatory Academy was intentionally located at the windward edge of campus to take full advantage of these predominant northern tradewinds. The building site faces due south towards the picturesque 14,000-foot Mauna Kea volcano. The due south exposure optimizes solar thermal and photovoltaic panel performance, and facilitates panoramic views from the interior of the building toward the volcano and valley below. The favorable Hawaiian climate and the building's dramatic hillside setting enable strong connections to the outdoors: an entry court is located to the east, a large teaching porch opens directly south, and a wind-sheltered court to the west supports a covered outdoor classroom.

Regional topography is reflected in the stepped, terraced arrangement of the building's internal spaces, where storage tanks, solar panels and other building systems have been strategically located to take advantage of this change in elevation. The resulting building is a single story, with a very high ceiling and high volume rooms. A large single classroom is at the center, with a large laboratory, smaller laboratory, and conference spaces at either edge. A large basement, known as the "Batcave", is used as a student shop. Batcave projects have included the iBoat, a small, remotely operated marine study vessel which monitored Hawaiian sea turtles and pollution levels within the nearby Pacific Ocean.

HPA includes open lattice doors that limit sunlight
while allowing fresh breezes into the building.

ENERGY STORY: ACHIEVING
NET ZERO AND BEYOND

With the building motto, "thinking about forever," the Energy Lab embodies conservation, providing an outlet for students to explore concepts in net zero energy, waste and water. The project team took a very thoughtful look at the program for the building and created a structure that responded to the climate and context of the site. When approaching the design of the Energy Lab, the team took multiple week-long site visits to experience the place, and consider the design and metrics from a variety of perspectives in open dialogue. Nearly half of the building pad is in outdoor alcoves and teaching spaces, which provide shading and wind shelter, recognizing the mild but windy climate of the building. The project was also an early pioneer in the use of computational fluid dynamic modeling for buildings, resulting in a significant evolution of the original design (discussed further below). The result is a building with a very effective wind driven ventilation system. Finally, a key lesson learned (also discussed further below) was in the weather data set, which turned out to be inaccurate relative to the site, and resulted in the overbuilding of the building's HVAC system. Regardless of this, the HPA building continues to be an inspiring ideal of designing with nature to yield a highly efficient, effective building. Indeed, for the purposes of drafting this case study, it was difficult to place different building elements into separate categories of system types, a testimony to the building's deeply integrated design.

HPA is a model case study in excellent daylighting.

DESIGN ELEMENTS

Envelope: Given the mild climate, the building envelope is fairly conventional. The walls are 2"x6" FSC certified wood framed with batt insulation infill, resulting in R-19. The roof is wood framed with rigid infill for a total of R-23. The windows are PPG Solarban 60, with a U-value of 0.29, solar heat gain coefficient of 0.38, and visible transmittance of 0.70. Translucent polycarbonate skylights allow diffused daylight into the space. Both the windows and the skylights minimize solar heat gain.

Cooling and Ventilation Design: The building was designed with a mixed mode cooling and ventilation system which combined simple and mechanized systems to provide a comfortable learning environment. This is consistent with the approach taken by most other mild climate cooling dominated buildings in this book. However, the HPA energy lab placed a proportionately greater emphasis on natural cooling, which influenced the overall design and form of the building.

The heart of cooling and ventilation efforts for the building (which in a typical school building in this climate zone would be the largest single energy load) is an innovative wind-driven ventilation system, which not only pushes air through the building but also pulls air through via a vacuum. As discussed above, a prevailing north wind blows from the Pacific Ocean over a high ridge to the Energy Lab, bringing cool air. Responding to this natural occurrence, the

Lab was designed with a single high roof peak running perpendicular to the wind. As the wind currents are forced up and over the roof peak, the air velocity increases. This action creates a natural vacuum on the back (south) side of the roof peak. This natural vacuum demonstrates Bernoulli's principle, discovered in the mid 1700s, which holds that increases in fluid velocity are accompanied by decreases in pressure in the area of the higher velocity. When cooling of the building is needed, automated louvers located just under the roof peak open allowing this natural, wind-driven vacuum to pull air up and out through the top of the building. Notably, the design team considered hopper windows as well as louvers at the upper clerestory to improve air movement. These options were eliminated because of the possibility of water infiltration under Kona wind conditions. Kona winds are infrequent but blow in the opposite direction to the prevailing trade winds.

The design team did not leave the details of this critical building element to chance. The team used computational fluid dynamic modeling to evaluate the effectiveness of

The building creates a myriad of usable outdoor spaces, allowing outdoor teaching throughout the day, depending on wind and sun direction.

the original building design, which proposed three lower height roof peaks. The modeling found that the design would not accelerate the wind enough to create the required vacuum. As a result, the design was changed to consolidate the three peaks into one taller peak. In actual function, the designed negative pressure system works very well, demonstrating the efficacy of the modeling.

The building responds to the wind and sun in a variety of other ways. Overall, the north side of the building creates an effective windblock: it contains only one set of low louvers to allow air flow, and is shaped to facilitate wind flow over the peak. Behind the north wall sits a variety of outdoor teaching spaces with vertical shading elements, allowing an array of choices depending on the strength of the wind and the location of the sun. Sliding wood slat shutters, which match the location of sliding glass doors, allow complete ventilation while minimizing solar heat gain and glare. The high ceilings allow the heat to stratify above the students as well.

The project also includes an experimental radiant cooling system. At night, water is circulated through thermal roof panels, and cooled via lower evening temperatures and radiance to the clear night sky. It is then stored in a 2,500 gallon below-grade tank for use as chilled water for air handling units during warm afternoons.

Mechanical 4.3 ton high efficiency SEER 16 air conditioners, as well as four ventilation fans, were included to provide overall back up to the more naturally-based systems. In practice, these systems have been used only very infrequently. (This is discussed further under the occupancy section below.)

Hot water is provided through a solar thermal system. Based on the mild climate, no heating was provided for the building.

Daylighting: Natural light was also carefully considered in the building design. The building's proximity to the equator results in a smaller range of seasonal daylight variances. A daylight simulation was created to ensure adequate daylight was available throughout the facility, without glare and high contrast, while minimizing solar heat gain. The result was very low artificial light usage, with only 114 kWh consumed for light in one year.

Monitoring: A computerized building management system monitors all aspects of the building, including temperature, humidity, CO_2, and occupancy, and regulates the systems accordingly, including operable windows and louvers and the mechanical HVAC system. Through this transparent monitoring, students of all ages can explore the relationship between energy, building conditions, and the climate around them. The system also monitors trends in weather, energy use, water use, solar output, ventilation, lighting and other metrics via a highly informative user interface. This becomes a deeply illuminating education tool that is then folded into the overall curriculum.

Renewable System: The Energy Lab is provided energy by three photovoltaic arrays for a total of 26.13 kW of solar power.

The three systems include:

North array: 10.8 kW array with 210 Watt Sanyo panels and Enphase microinverters.

Central array: 12.6 kW array with Sanyo 210 Watt panels, feeding 2 x 6 kW SMA inverters.

South array/solar awning: 2.73 kW from 14 Sanyo bifacial 195 Watt PV panels, providing light below and absorbing light in both directions (up and down), feeding into a 3 kW SMA inverter. Because these panels absorb light on both faces, they are 22 percent efficient, higher than the typical 17-18 percent.

OCCUPANCY AND LESSONS LEARNED

In practice, the mechanical cooling systems of the building turned out to be unnecessary and are used only very occasionally. This system miscalculation was due in large part to the nearest available meteorological data being from the Hilo Airport, nearly fifty miles from the site. This data was used as the basis for the main energy model for the project. It turns out the Hilo Airport sits at sea level, and is in an entirely different climate zone than the site. The predicted versus actual weather and insolation differed. (For example, the average predicted temperature was 73.6 degrees F, versus the 65.1 degrees F actually observed.) Insolation was higher than predicted, resulting in better solar photovoltaic output, and wind speed was less, allowing windows to be left open more frequently. (A concern during the design process was that wind speeds would be high enough to require windows to stay closed, resulting in thermal gain within the lab.) An additional problem with the HVAC mechanical system is that visiting classes occasionally turn it on with the windows and louvers open and do not turn it off, and there is no simple remote or automated system for shutting it down.

The passive system itself has proved very successful over time, but one comment is that the upper vent windows are top hinged, meaning the window actually blocks the airflow adjacent to the strongest point of vacuum. Dr. Bill Wiecking, the Energy Lab Director, suggests that an improved design would use a louvered window instead.

Another finding has been that the passive system vents heat well, but not necessarily CO_2 because CO_2 is heavier than O_2 and N_2, and thus tends to sink within an enclosed space. The HPA vents sit at the top of the space, which bypasses this low-lying CO_2. The school is considering installing a lower vent or fan based vent/mixing element to remedy this situation.

HOOD RIVER MIDDLE SCHOOL MUSIC AND SCIENCE BUILDING

HOOD RIVER, OR, USA

PROJECT TEAM

OWNER: Hood River County School District

ARCHITECT: Opsis Architecture

CONTRACTOR: Kirby Nagelhout

MECHANICAL, ELECTRICAL, AND PLUMBING ENGINEER: Interface Engineering

LIGHTING: Interface Engineering

CIVIL ENGINEER: KPFF Consulting Engineers

STRUCTURAL ENGINEER: KPFF Consulting Engineers

COMMISSIONING: McKinstry

LANDSCAPE ARCHITECT: Green Works PC

SIZE:
1 floor / 5,328 sf

BUILDING FOOTPRINT:
5,134 sf

SITE:
42,754 sf

TYPE:
Building (Public Middle School)

LIVING TRANSECT:
L3, Village or Campus Zone

WEBSITE:
opsisarch.com/wp-content/uploads/2012/05/Hood-River-Detailed-Sustainable-Case-Study.pdf

LOCATION:
Hood River, OR, USA

EUI:
26.7 kBtu/sf/yr

PV SIZE:
35 kW

OTHER RENEWABLES:
2,000 CFM transpired solar collector

CLIMATE ZONE:
Cold

ANNUAL ENERGY USE:
ACTUAL:
41,811 kWh

SIMULATED/DESIGNED:
37,062 kWh

CONSTRUCTION COST:
$233/sf

CERTIFICATION:
ILFI-Certified Net Zero Energy Building

DATE CERTIFIED:
May 2014

Hood River Middle School's net zero energy Music and Science Building was designed and built to create a space that exemplifies sustainable design as a learning tool with its Outdoor Classroom Project, and to blend the school's future with the school's historic past. The Music and Science Building includes music rooms, practice rooms, teacher offices, a science lab and a greenhouse. The 5,328 square foot multipurpose classroom features several innovative components, including utilizing local stream water for cooling, insulated concrete forms, and a thermal air heating plenum to warm incoming ventilation air. The blending of education through discovery was the impetus in combining green building, permaculture principles, sciences and music into the same learning center.

The school, which is listed on the U.S. National Register of Historic Places, is located along Oregon's Columbia River, east of Portland, on a nine-acre parcel of land, with over 21,000 square feet of open space and a view of Mount Adams. The building's greenhouse serves as a laboratory where students grow plants using water from a "living machine" that recycles wastewater for irrigation. The students' growing and harvesting efforts also serve the larger community: every Thursday students participate in the Gorge Grown Farmers' Market hosted at the school.

148

The Hood River Middle School used integrated concrete forms for the walls, demonstrating yet another technique for a high insulation value envelope. Photo: Opsis Architecture

DESIGN ELEMENTS

Envelope: A solid envelope was critical to the large, multifunctional learning space, keeping students and faculty comfortable year-round. Insulated concrete formwork walls (ICFs) achieve an overall R-value of 25, and provide excellent thermal mass, buffering against Hood River's seasonal temperature swings. The Hood River Middle School (HRMS) Music and Science Building is the only Net Zero Energy certified building to use ICFs, and is an exemplary model of their appropriate use given the local climate with frequent wide daily temperature swings. This type of wall uses polystyrene foam interlocking blocks

FINANCING

Soft costs:	$485,000
Hard costs:	$1,240,000
Price per square foot:	$233
PV system design and installation:	$227,000
Public incentives (state, local, federal):	$154,000*
Private incentives:	None
TOTAL PROJECT COST (excluding land purchase):	**$1,700,000**

*The Energy Trust of Oregon Path to Net-Zero Pilot Project provided monetary incentives totalling $15,000 for energy efficiency and $45,000 for renewable energy. The State of Oregon provided the project with a Business Energy Tax Credit LEED Platinum Incentive of $13,600 and a BETC Photovoltaic Incentive of $80,400. Project incentives came to a total of $154,000.

to construct the formwork for the walls. Concrete was then poured in stages into the formwork with rebar used for added structural stability. The forms were left in place to add to the building's thermal protection layer. The monolithic nature of ICFs, combined with proper detailing, drastically reduces air infiltration and thermal bridging. Lapped rigid insulation (R-38) was used in the roof and under the radiant concrete floors (R-15). The windows' wooden frames are higher in thermal resistance than the aluminum frames typically found at schools, and feature triple glazing to prevent extra heat gain and loss.

Heating, Cooling, and Ventilation: The building uses a well integrated system of heating, cooling, and ventilation which thoughtfully uses natural systems that come to the site. The principal heating and cooling system for the project is ground source heat pumps. The main ground source prewarming loop is a horizontal system located ten feet under the soccer field adjacent to the school. Water from the nearby tributary of the Columbia River provides cooling water for the heat pump in the summer months, and is also used for landscape irrigation. Heating/cooling distribution is provided via

tubes in a radiant concrete floor. Natural ventilation is comprised of a cross and stack ventilation system, allowing air to move through low and high clerestory windows. A red-green light monitor notifies the occupants when outside temperatures are comfortable, and CO_2 levels are too high for natural ventilation—one of the many ways students interact with the building as a learning lab. When outdoor temperatures are outside of the comfort range, a mechanical heat recovery ventilator system operates, bringing in heat transferred ventilation air in combination with fans, distributing the air throughout

INTEGRATED DESIGN

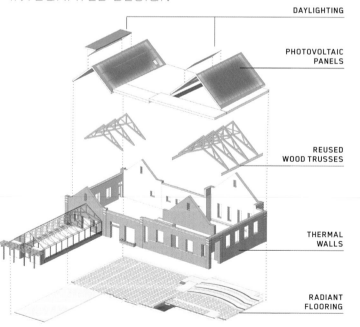

DAYLIGHTING

PHOTOVOLTAIC
PANELS

REUSED
WOOD TRUSSES

THERMAL
WALLS

RADIANT
FLOORING

THE POWER OF ZERO

the classroom. An innovative prewarming solar electric heat collector is routed to the HRV, which further increases its efficiency. The collector is constructed on an angled plenum on the roof, that sits under the solar panels that generate heat when they are producing electricity. By removing the heat, the solar panels also operate more efficiently, doubling the benefit.

Lighting and miscellaneous: The windows, in addition to translucent skylights and clerestory windows, also allow for substantial daylight. To prevent spikes in plug loads, dual operation outlets shut off when the building is not in use, as determined by occupant sensors.

Renewables: The HRMS building utilizes a grid-tied 35-kW photovoltaic array of 165 Sanyo HIT 215N modules on a net-metering plan with the electric utility, Pacific Power. The arrays are architecturally integrated on south facing gabled roofs, providing optimal solar angles, with a small number of panels mounted horizontally. Early data showed that the actual energy generation exceeded projections by nearly 17 percent, at 42,363 kWh. It appears the simulated data was based on general area weather information that might not have factored in the site's microclimate, potentially contributing to the higher performance.

EUI: HOOD RIVER MIDDLE SCHOOL MUSIC AND SCIENCE BUILDING

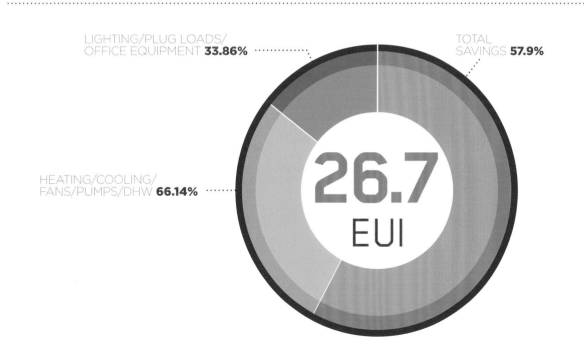

LIGHTING/PLUG LOADS/ OFFICE EQUIPMENT **33.86%**

TOTAL SAVINGS **57.9%**

HEATING/COOLING/ FANS/PUMPS/DHW **66.14%**

26.7 EUI

57.9% SAVINGS FROM BASELINE

63.4 KBTU/SF/YEAR BASELINE EUI*

* ASHRAE 90.1 – 2007, Primary school category, all climates

SACRED HEART LOWER AND MIDDLE SCHOOL STEVENS LIBRARY

ATHERTON, CALIFORNIA,
USA

The Sacred Heart School (SHS) Lower and Middle School campus includes four new buildings arranged around a large landscaped space to preserve existing heritage oak trees. These buildings include two classroom spaces, a performing arts and assembly hall, and the Stevens Library. Built on a 11,935 square foot site, the Stevens Library is a 6,800 square foot, ILFI-Certified Net Zero Energy Building with an EUI of 16.9 kBtu/sf. Located in the San Francisco Bay Area town of Atherton, in heart of the Silicon Valley, the K-8 campus library reflects the sustainable and educational values of the school. A goal of the new campus construction was to be a carbon neutral, net zero energy building that would be a great teaching tool for the students. The Stevens LIbrary is a Pacific Gas & Electric Net Zero Pilot Project, which enables third party metering and monitoring as well as technical support. Flexibility is a key feature of the Stevens Library that seeks to accommodate a variety of ages and learning styles, with modifiable furniture and spaces. The library was built and certified at roughly the same time as the West Berkeley Public Library (see page 160), offering an interesting comparison between two similar, yet different, buildings and occupancies.

(see page 160)

SIZE:
1 floor / 6,800 sf

BUILDING FOOTPRINT:
6,800 sf

SITE:
11,935 sf

TYPE:
Education Campus

LIVING TRANSECT:
L3, Village or Campus Zone

WEBSITE:
shschools.org

LOCATION:
Atherton, California, USA

EUI:
16.9 kBtu/sf/yr

PV SIZE:
42.5 kW

OTHER RENEWABLES:
None

CLIMATE ZONE:
Marine

ANNUAL ENERGY USE:
ACTUAL ENERGY USE:
26,687 kWh

ACTUAL ELECTRICITY GENERATED:
53,188 kWh

NET ENERGY GENERATION:
26,501.4kWh

CONSTRUCTION COST:
$353/sf

CERTIFICATION:
ILFI-Certified Net Zero Energy Building

DATE CERTIFIED:
November 2014

153

154

The Sacred Heart Library used a form of displacement ventilation that uses the interior itself as part of the ventilation conveyance and simplifies mechanical systems.

The primary mission of this high-visibility campus hub is to teach students about being stewards of the planet. In support of that mission, a key goal was to display the ways in which its construction and daily operations contribute to the school's ethos of conservation and stewardship. The project team's motivation to design and build a Net Zero Energy library was to create a building independent of fossil fuels, committed to resource reduction, and dedicated to a healthy environment. Today, the Stevens Library—a light-filled, healthy, flexible learning environment—enhances the vitality of the 10.4-acre school campus.

The Sacred Heart Schools sought an open, flexible learning environment that would accommodate traditional library functions while supporting cross-disciplinary and project-based learning, small group work, digital learning, and informal gathering. The school also wanted to create an outdoor learning environment where students could experience a hands-on connection to nature. The library is designed so that 90 percent of the spaces are flexible: simple counters allow for mobile furniture storage underneath, permitting easy adaptation of the spaces, and the furniture is designed to serve a wide range of ages. These flexible features accommodate a multitude of educational, administrative and community needs. The design team's discussions with the client on topics of "double duty" and flexibility resulted in an 8 percent reduction in total square footage and a decrease in overall expense. The Stevens Library is a Net Zero Energy Building Certified by the International Living Future Institute and LEED® Platinum through the US Green Building Council. The project was designed and constructed at 20 percent below industry standard prices, proving that advanced sustainable design can also be affordable design.

FINANCING

Soft costs:	$200,000*
Hard costs:	$2,400,000**
Price per square foot:	$353***
Public incentives (state, local, federal):	None
Private sources:	Private donations
TOTAL PROJECT COST (excluding land purchase):	**$2,600,000**

*Not including design

**Part of larger campus construction/bid effort

***Hard cost only

The completely flat solar array has proved difficult to keep clean; some array tilt allows the panels to self clean when rainfall occurs.

ENERGY STORY:
ACHIEVING NET ZERO AND BEYOND

The library is located in the very mild climate of the Bay Area, where the Pacific Ocean and San Francisco Bay provide a moderating influence on temperatures, and also generate a significant amount of wind, which can aid with cooling. Little extra funding was available to achieve net zero energy, so the overall building design and supporting systems were kept relatively simple. Outside the building, tree canopies provide shading, and a garden extends the indoor space to the outdoors as a living classroom. There are large windows on the north and south sides of the building that allow for spacious views and daylight for reading and learning exercises. The project is mixed-mode, taking advantage of natural ventilation in all spaces.

The project team coupled good building orientation with studies of the site including weather profiles and wind pattern studies, with the help of radiance, sun and shade modeling by SketchUp, eQuest, and Ecotect Analysis. In practice, the building energy use was significantly lower than modeled.

DESIGN ELEMENTS:

Envelope: Reflective of the mild climate, the building envelope exceeds code but is not as insulated as many NZE buildings in other climate zones. The Stevens Library has metal framing, 24 inches on center, to reduce cost. Batt insulation within the frame, and an additional 1-inch of rigid insulation outside the frame provide a thermal break to the highly thermally conductive metal framing, resulting in a wall R-value of R-15. The roof includes insulation within the joists, in addition to 2 inches of rigid insulation on top of the decking, for a total of R-38. The roof is white to reduce thermal gain in this predominantly cooling-driven building. The windows feature a Solarban 70XL glazing—a high performance double glazing with a U-value of 0.28 and a solar heat gain coefficient of 0.28—reducing solar gain in the summer but retaining necessary heat in the winter. A large southwest facing section of glass, also the main building entry, is deeply recessed into the building façade, providing an elegant way to allow multiple functions: an architectural delineation of the entrance, a covered entry, and direct shading onto the glass which prevents thermal gain on this critical aspect. Careful insulation installation and air sealing limited air leakage.

HVAC: The primary HVAC load on the building is cooling, and given the mild climate, the building was thoughtfully designed to provide just enough cooling based on the least energy intensive source available. Cool air is provided through an economizer cycle on an air handler, drawing in unconditioned outside air when it meets interior temperature needs; openable windows also provide this function. Additionally, the building uses a package cooling unit that combines an evaporative cooling cycle and a heat pump-type compressor for higher loads. This unit stages its output to provide cool air using evaporative cooling first, and then during very hot days activating the compressor. The net benefit of this system is that it stages up to provide cooling, rather than using a single energy intensive component to provide small cooling increments.

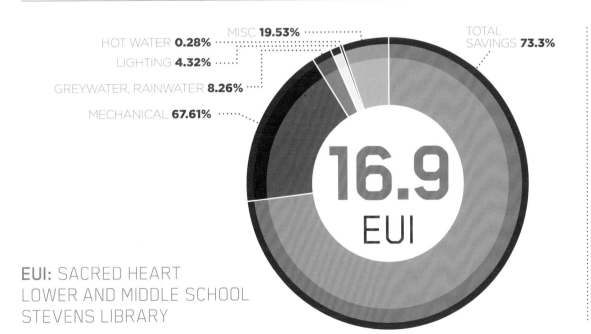

HOT WATER **0.28%**
MISC **19.53%**
LIGHTING **4.32%**
GREYWATER, RAINWATER **8.26%**
MECHANICAL **67.61%**
TOTAL SAVINGS **73.3%**

16.9 EUI

EUI: SACRED HEART LOWER AND MIDDLE SCHOOL STEVENS LIBRARY

73.3%
SAVINGS FROM BASELINE

63.4
KBTU/SF/YEAR BASELINE EUI*

* ASHRAE 90.1 – 2007,
Primary school category,
all climates

RENEWABLES PROFILE: PHOTOVOLTAIC ARRAY

The photovoltaic system—comprised of 170 modules at 250 watts per panel—covers the majority of the rooftop, and results in a 42.5 kW system. The roof-mounted panels are SolarWorld Sunmodule SW250 mono version 2.0. The system's direct current is converted to alternating current via a single large Satcon Power Gate Plus 50kW inverter. The 42.5 kW system shares the building roof with the packaged HVAC unit and the solar tube collectors.

The solar photovoltaic panels are mounted without tilt primarily to avoid shading of one panel by another in the densely-packed array. That arrangement was also preferred by the local building agency because an unfortunate local ordinance from the 1970s restricts visible solar panel arrays on buildings. Drawbacks of the horizontal layout are a 17 percent reduction in production efficiency, as well as increased cleaning requirements due to lack of self-cleaning during rainfall. Though hidden from the street, the panels are visible to students from the second floor of the classroom building, a benefit to the educational goals of the project.

The system was sized to fill out the available roof space, with the understanding that the actual building demand would deviate from the predicted annual consumption of 50,361 kWh. The energy modeling results indicated that the 42.5 kW system would be more than sufficient to produce net zero energy performance. This prediction is supported by the measured results.

The ventilation system consists of operable windows and a displacement ventilation system. Displacement ventilation, commonplace in Europe (particularly Nordic countries), takes a simplified approach which uses the building itself as a thermal mixing element. Fresh air, conditioned if necessary, is blown into the space, typically at the floor level. This places the building under a slight positive pressure. The cool air then mixes within the space and exits via dedicated vents. No return ducting is provided, and supply ducting is minimal, reducing space demands and cost. The Stevens Library displacement system is unusual in that the supply is provided by air nozzles mounted at the ceiling and pointed downward. (Typically, displacement air is brought in at the floor.) Additional circulation and air movement is provided by ceiling fans, further providing a sense of cool and air movement.

Daylighting: To reduce artificial lighting needs, the building incorporates daylighting, solar tubes and skylights in addition to operable windows, oriented to maximize light and prevent solar thermal gain for most of the building throughout the year. The solar tubes, made by Solatube, use the same refractive Fresnel collectors and diffusers used in the DPR Phoenix building (see page 88). Daylighting is monitored with sensors which respond to changing light levels and turn on the low power lighting system when necessary. This low power system is also monitored with occupancy sensors.

Energy monitoring: Energy monitors display performance on screens visible to students and faculty, giving instant feedback about their actions. The successfully low energy use is connected to occupant behavior, with students, faculty and staff consciously reducing their use of resources and learning how to correctly use a net zero energy building.

OCCUPANCY

The team learned important lessons during the performance period. In actual use, the building requires far less energy than predicted: 24,384 kWh actual versus the 50,361 kWh modeled. The most significant lesson to emerge was that it is necessary to spend more time on the details of the energy model during both design and construction. The divergence was attributed to three general areas:

1. The use of hot water and assumed overall occupancy was overestimated.

2. The use of lighting was overestimated due to a modeling software limitation.

3. The incorporation of the greywater tank and systems into the plug loads was not considered during modeling since these elements are part of an overall campus system. Because the pumps are tied to the building meter, it was determined that this load should be attributed to the library. This resulted in an increased building EUI.

WEST BERKELEY PUBLIC LIBRARY

BERKELEY, CA, USA

PROJECT TEAM

OWNER:
City of Berkeley

ARCHITECT:
Harley Ellis Devereaux

**GENERAL
CONTRACTOR:**
West Bay Builders

**MECHANICAL,
ELECTRICAL, AND
PLUMBING ENGINEER:**
Timmons Design

**STRUCTURAL
ENGINEER:**
TippingMar

**GEOTECHNICAL AND
CIVIL ENGINEER:**
Moran Engineering

COMMISSIONING:
Orry Nottingham

LIGHTING DESIGN:
Max Pierson

**LANDSCAPE
ARCHITECT:**
John North Roberts
& Associates

**SPECIALTY
CONSULTANTS:**
Harley Ellis
Devereaux/
Greenworks, SFMI,
Bruning Associates

SIZE:
2 floors / 9,399 sf

BUILDING FOOTPRINT:
8,920 sf

SITE:
11,970 sf

TYPE:
Public Building

LIVING TRANSECT:
L4, General Urban Zone

WEBSITE:
berkeleypubliclibrary.org/
locations/west-branch

LOCATION:
Berkeley, CA, USA

EUI:
24.1 kBtu/sf/yr

PV SIZE:
52 kW (120 SunPower
E20/435 panels)

OTHER RENEWABLES:
A solar thermal system
(supplemented by electric heat
pumps) tied directly to the
radiant slab system provides
heating for the building

CLIMATE ZONE:
Marine

CONSTRUCTION COST:
$617/sf

CERTIFICATION:
ILFI-Certified Net Zero
Energy Building

DATE CERTIFIED:
March 2014

The City of Berkeley created an ambitious climate action plan in 2009, with an overarching goal to reduce the city's greenhouse gas emissions to 33 percent below 2000 levels by 2020. As part of meeting this goal, city buildings would need to be updated, and accordingly, a measure was passed in 2008 to retrofit libraries in the municipality for high efficiency energy use. Architecture and engineering firm Harley Ellis Devereaux (HED) won the bid as the only firm to propose that the West Berkeley Public Library strive to be a net zero energy building. West Berkeley is the first NZE public library, providing a highly visible, state-of-the-art facility for the surrounding community.

From a design standpoint, the building is notable for its thoughtfully staged passive and active cooling system, including a wind chimney that creates natural vacuums to draw air through the structure. The building also has no parking, instead encouraging walking, biking, and transit use. The library includes open book stacks, several public seating areas, a community room, a computer training lab, and staff offices and support rooms. The 9,399 square foot library opened in December 2013 and received ILFI-certified Net Zero Energy Building status in March 2014.

FINANCING

Soft costs:	$1,947,445*
Hard costs:	$5,797,653
Price per square foot:	$617
Public incentives (state, local, federal):	PG&E Savings by Design program
Private incentives:	None
TOTAL PROJECT COST (excluding land purchase):	**$7,514,445**

*$537,320 FF&E costs separate from project budget

A busy, well-used urban library has higher occupant loads than might be expected.

ENERGY STORY: ACHIEVING NET ZERO AND BEYOND

The library is located in the mild climate of the San Francisco Bay Area, and uses passive design to take advantage of ample wind and sun on-site. The collaborative nature of the design process had HED Architects engaging with the community from the start, through workshops aimed at creating a space that was inviting and desirable. The following extensive building simulation, modeling and research was carried out by in-house HED/Greenworks team members:

- Site and climate analysis

- Plug load, energy usage and available renewable energy generation analysis

- Solar insolation studies to determine the optimum roof height for maximum solar gain and minimal solar access encroachment

- Computational fluid dynamics modeling to study the effectiveness of a wind chimney in drawing fresh air through the building

- Thermal comfort verification of staff offices and adult literacy area

- Daylighting studies

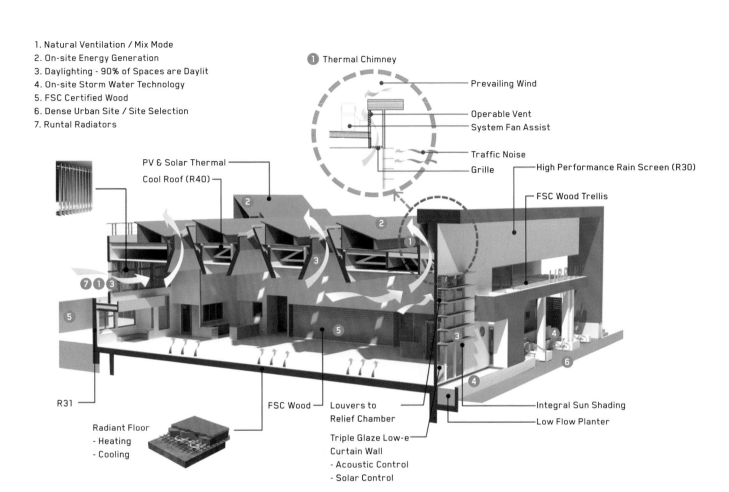

1. Natural Ventilation / Mix Mode
2. On-site Energy Generation
3. Daylighting - 90% of Spaces are Daylit
4. On-site Storm Water Technology
5. FSC Certified Wood
6. Dense Urban Site / Site Selection
7. Runtal Radiators

1 Thermal Chimney

Prevailing Wind

Operable Vent
System Fan Assist

Traffic Noise
Grille

High Performance Rain Screen (R30)

FSC Wood Trellis

PV & Solar Thermal
Cool Roof (R40)

R31

FSC Wood — Louvers to Relief Chamber

Triple Glaze Low-e Curtain Wall
- Acoustic Control
- Solar Control

Radiant Floor
- Heating
- Cooling

Integral Sun Shading
Low Flow Planter

DESIGN ELEMENTS

Envelope: To achieve high efficiency with a large, yet varying amount of occupants, the West Berkeley Public Library required an envelope that is both flexible and functionally suited to the mild San Francisco Bay Area climate. The building is assembled with 3"x8" wood studs, 24 inches on center, and 1-inch plywood sheathing. The envelope was designed to be vapor permeable, and uses an Enershield HP water barrier. The roof assembly is 1-inch plywood sheathing over either I-joists of varying depths or wood trusses at the skylights. Roxul mineral wool is used for wall and ceiling insulation, resulting in R-31 for the walls and R-40 in the roof. The building's variety of exterior finishes assist the water barrier and control thermal conditions based on the position to the elements. The south side is sided with cement boards mounted over the plywood sheathing to function as a rain screen.

For the west, north and east sides of the library, a ⅞" cement plaster is used. R-9 rigid insulation is also present between the radiant concrete floor and a structural matt slab.

HVAC: Heating and cooling is provided through a sophisticated system which combines active and passive techniques. The building uses a thoughtfully designed elevated stack vent along the south edge of the structure (behind the primary street-facing façade). This

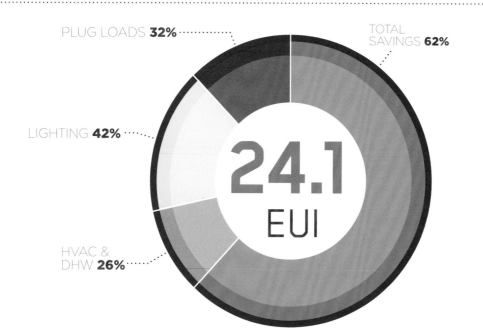

PLUG LOADS **32%**

LIGHTING **42%**

HVAC & DHW **26%**

TOTAL SAVINGS **62%**

24.1 EUI

62% SAVINGS FROM BASELINE

63.4 KBTU/SF/YEAR BASELINE EUI*

* ASHRAE 90.1 – 2007, Primary school category, all climates

vent allows wind driven and stack negative pressure driven airflow to move through the building, at times without mechanical assistance.

Flat plate solar thermal collectors are located on the roof, providing heat to a radiant slab. If there's insufficient sunlight, supplementary heating, as well as mechanical cooling, is provided via three small air-to-air heat pumps located on the roof. Required air exchanges are achieved with fresh incoming air passing through radiators at the exterior windows. These operable windows are opened and closed by the Building Management System (BMS), which utilizes sensors within each space to detect elevated levels of carbon dioxide. Windows can be opened manually for added individual control, but the BMS closes the windows as necessary to ensure energy is not wasted.

The library uses a staged cooling system, conceptually similar to DPR Construction's Regional Phoenix Office building (see page 88), which scales up depending on outside temperatures and internal occupancies heating the space:

Cooling mode 1: In the cool, early season, outside air is drawn through the building, utilizing negative pressure at the wind chimney to extract warm interior air. Typically, air flow arrives via the north operable windows, flows through the building, and up the wind chimney. In addition to carbon dioxide sensors, there are thermostats within each space or zone that monitor the temperature of the room and communicate with the BMS. Should the temperature exceed or fall below set points, the radiant system will initiate.

Cooling Mode 2: In moderately warm temperatures, Cooling Mode 1 is employed, plus additional air movement is achieved by opening operable skylights.

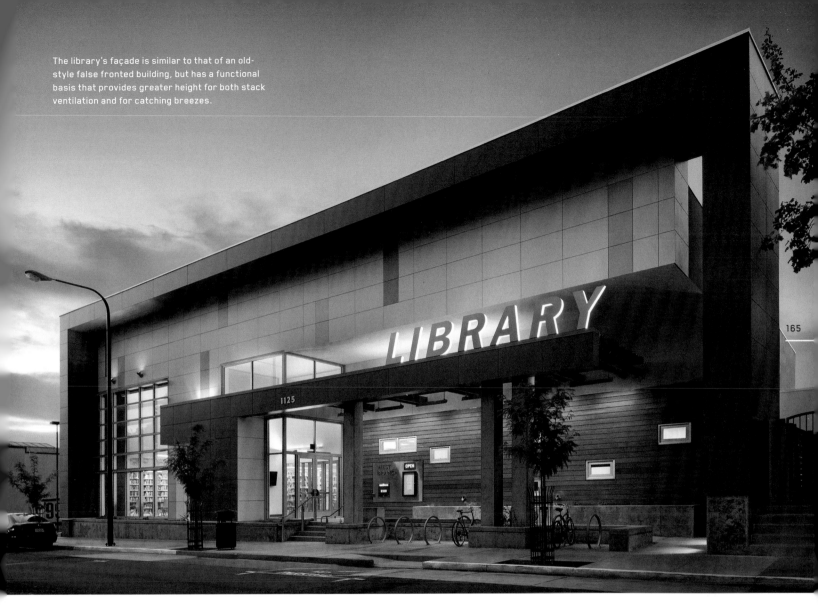

The library's façade is similar to that of an old-style false fronted building, but has a functional basis that provides greater height for both stack ventilation and for catching breezes.

Cooling Mode 3: During warm weather, Cooling Modes 1 & 2 are used, with additional air movement utilizing large fans in interior spaces, and a supplementary exhaust fan located at the wind chimney for heat extraction.

Cooling Mode 4: In hot temperatures, all windows and skylights are shut. Supplementary cooling is provided through the radiant floor via heat pumps and a condensing unit on the roof. Windows are opened by BMS for fresh air intake as required. Additional internal ventilation is provided through exhaust fans located in the restrooms and other main rooms at the library (computer lab, study rooms), with ducts to exchange air between smaller and larger spaces. A transfer chamber regulates air movement between the library book stacks and staffing areas.

Lighting: The windows and skylights provide high quality daylighting; however, as a library needs sufficient light for reading and working, the artificial lighting is tied to sensors, which dims the lighting as appropriate.

In practice, daylight provides 95 percent of the needed interior light during daylight hours.

Occupancy loads: Plug loads are carefully monitored at the site with a reduced number of strategically located outlets, and a laptop checkout program that allows staff to monitor charging use.

Renewables: The West Berkeley Public Library utilizes a 120 panel SunPower E20/435 system, providing 52 kw of peaking power. The SunPower panels, also used on the Bullitt Center (see page 102), are the most efficient on the market, about 10-20 percent better than typical solar panels, by utilizing a proprietary design which places diodes behind the silicon, eliminating that shading impact. The photovoltaic-generated direct current is converted to alternating current by a single Aurora PVI Central inverter, located inside in a mechanical equipment mezzanine. The rooftop panels are split into four arrays facing south alongside the solar thermal system which assists in building thermal regulation. Rather than using typical flat roof rack mounts, the PV's are mounted on a custom designed and fabricated rack/stanchion system that allows future re-roofing as well as consistent height.

OCCUPANCY

In practice, the West Berkeley library is a humming, busy urban community gathering place, open to the public 52 hours a week (even longer when taking into account staff preparation and after hours activities). Public libraries, particularly in urban settings, have changed over the years, becoming less places for book storage and checkout, and more a combination of reading room, mobile workplace, and day shelter for the homeless. These realities mean there are more users within libraries, who engage in more activities than the past practice of finding books, checking them out, and leaving. User loads at West Berkeley Public Library have been higher than expected, due in large part to extensive laptop charging by visitors. Based on the lighting submetering information, it also appears that lights are left on during the nighttime, likely for security.

WEST BERKELEY
VS. SACRED HEART

The construction and certification of two similarly sized libraries in the same climate zone and locale, one with an EUI of 24.1 kBtu/sf and the other of 16.9, yet with similar levels of energy saving design and technologies, raises the question: Why the difference?

167

A review of the submetering information is informative. Both buildings have roughly the same HVAC usage. However, the West Berkeley Library has dramatically higher occupant and lighting loads. At closer investigation, this is hardly surprising—the Sacred Heart Library is open substantially fewer hours since it follows the school calendar and is closed holiday weeks and during the summer. Perhaps even more importantly, the West Berkeley Library has plug loads introduced by users, in particular, laptop charging, and it has more employees. West Berkeley also includes a computer training lab with a number of permanent computers that also draw loads. In general, spaces with an array of staffing and visitors, such as West Berkeley, have a harder time limiting user loads than those with more regular occupants, such as Sacred Heart.

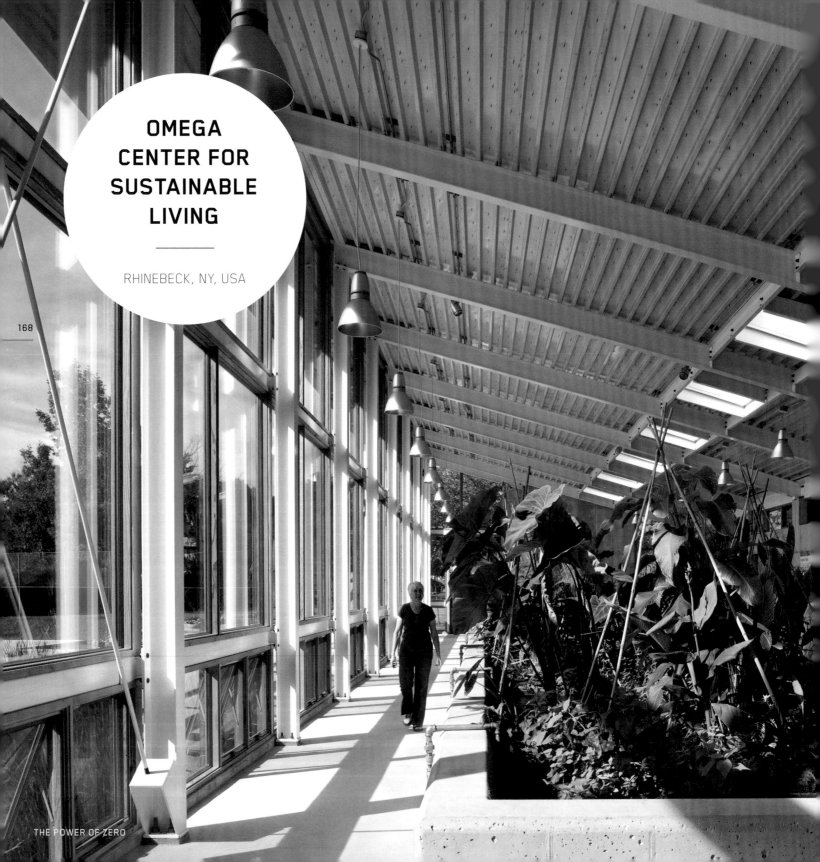

OMEGA CENTER FOR SUSTAINABLE LIVING

RHINEBECK, NY, USA

PROJECT TEAM

OWNER:
Omega Institute for
Holistic Studies,Inc

ARCHITECT:
BNIM Architects

CONTRACTOR:
David Sember
Construction

**MECHANICAL
ENGINEER:**
BGR Consulting
Engineers

**ELECTRICAL
ENGINEER:**
BGR Consulting
Engineers

**PLUMBING
ENGINEER:**
BGR Consulting
Engineers

**INTERIOR
DESIGN:**
BNIM Architects

**ECOLOGICAL
DESIGN:**
John Todd
Ecological Design

SIZE:
1 floor / 6,246 sf

SITE:
141,350 sf

TYPE:
Building/Educational

LIVING TRANSECT:
L3, Village or Campus Zone

WEBSITE:
eomega.org/visit-us/
rhinebeck-ny

LOCATION:
Rhinebeck, NY, USA

EUI:
20.3 kBtu/sf/year

PV SIZE:
48.53 kW PV array (located
on roof, trellis, and wall)

OTHER RENEWABLES:
None

CLIMATE ZONE:
Cold

ANNUAL ENERGY USE:
ACTUAL:
37,190 kWh

ELECTRICITY GENERATED:
38,994 kWh

TOTAL DESIGN OUTPUT:
46,305 kW

CONSTRUCTION COST:
$672/sf

CERTIFICATION:
Full Living Building Challenge
Certified; ILFI-certified
Net Zero Energy Building

DATE CERTIFIED:
October 2010

The **Omega Center for Sustainable Living (OCSL) is an advanced wastewater treatment center and educational space that is part of the Omega Institute for Holistic Studies in Rhinebeck, New York.** Situated in the beautiful Hudson River Valley, the building incorporates visible elements of the wastewater treatment system as an advanced commitment to sustainability. A 48.53 kW photovoltaic array powers the complex wastewater processing system and additional needs of the OCSL. The building, designed by BNIM Architects, was commissioned by the Omega Institute to replace a failing community-scale septic system and to treat the wastewater for its 195 acre learning and retreat center. The water is treated through the Eco Machine™, a nature-mimicking technology process designed by John Todd, a leader in ecological design. (The process uses no chemicals; only microscopic algae, fungi, bacteria, plants, and snails are used for purification.) All reclaimed water is then used for irrigating gardens around the grounds. The Center for Sustainable Living functions as an educational space where the Omega Center hosts various sustainability initiatives, as well as specialized classes on wastewater management.

The south facing façade and eaves were designed to maximize winter solar gain and limit summer overheating. The resulting roof form faces north, resulting in the solar array being ground mounted.

FINANCING

Soft costs:	N/A
Hard costs:	N/A
Price per square foot:	$672
Public incentives (state, local, federal):	$200,000*
Private incentives:	None
TOTAL PROJECT COST (excluding land purchase):	**$4,200,000**

*PON 2112 - NY-Sun Solar Electric Incentive Program from New York State Energy Research and Development Authority (NYSERDA)

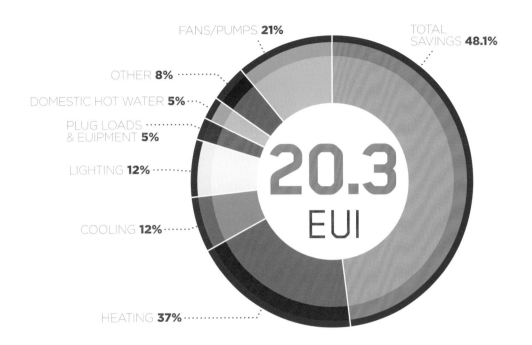

FANS/PUMPS **21%**

OTHER **8%**

DOMESTIC HOT WATER **5%**

PLUG LOADS
& EQUIPMENT **5%**

LIGHTING **12%**

COOLING **12%**

HEATING **37%**

TOTAL
SAVINGS **48.1%**

20.3
EUI

48.1%
SAVINGS FROM
BASELINE

39.1
KBTU/SF/YEAR
BASELINE EUI*

*ASHRAE 90.1 – 2007,
Small office category,
all climates

171

ENERGY STORY:
ACHIEVING NET ZERO
AND BEYOND

The building uses passive and mechanical
strategies to meet its heating, cooling, and
lighting needs. The overall design of the
south-facing eaves and windows allows
thermal gain within the space during the
cold—yet sunny—winters of the area, while
preventing overheating during the summer
by shading direct sunlight on windows.
Additional heating and cooling is provided
through a ground source heat pump system.

Concrete helps
stabilize internal
temperatures.

DESIGN ELEMENTS

Envelope: The envelope has R-33 walls and
an R-31 roof. The walls are insulated with
5.5 inches of batt fiberglass insulation and 2
inches of polyisocyanurate insulation, while
the roof has 5 inches of polyisocyanurate
insulation. The south-facing windows are
high performance double-paned Cardinal
179 with special coatings, with a low U-value
of 0.28 and a high solar heat gain coefficient
of 0.70. The remaining windows are Cardinal

270 double-paned, with a 0.25 U-value and
0.37 solar heat gain coefficient. Additionally,
a green roof keeps the space cooler during
the summer months, as well as providing
additional insulation. The thermal activity
of the Eco Machine™ provides additional
heating at times as well as a tempering effect
on temperature swings, which is further
supported by the thermal mass of the concrete
construction of much of the building.

HVAC: A ground source heat pump system
provides primary heating and cooling for the

North facing skylights provide indirect light inside the space.

173

building, with a total of four heat pumps dedicated to different portions of the building. Distribution of heating and cooling is a combination of hydronic and blown air, with water-based heating/cooling provided to the sewage lagoon and classroom floor, and air-based heating/cooling to the foyer, bathroom, and classroom.

Daylighting: The space is very well daylit, with an expansive south-facing glass array as well as north facing windows and skylights. Supplemental lighting is fluorescent, with vacancy sensors.

Renewables: The OCSL features three solar PV arrays mounted on the roof, walls and trellis consisting of 211 SunPower 230 watt modules and 8 SunPower inverters. The 48.52 kW system is located around the building: on the wall-mounted awning, the roof, and a second outdoor classroom array. All of the systems feed into the space's electricity room, which is grid-tied through a net metering agreement, selling excess power to the local utility, Central Hudson Gas & Electric. The system was supported by The New York State Energy Research and Development Authority (NYSERDA) under the NY-Sun Solar Electric Incentive Program for $200,000.

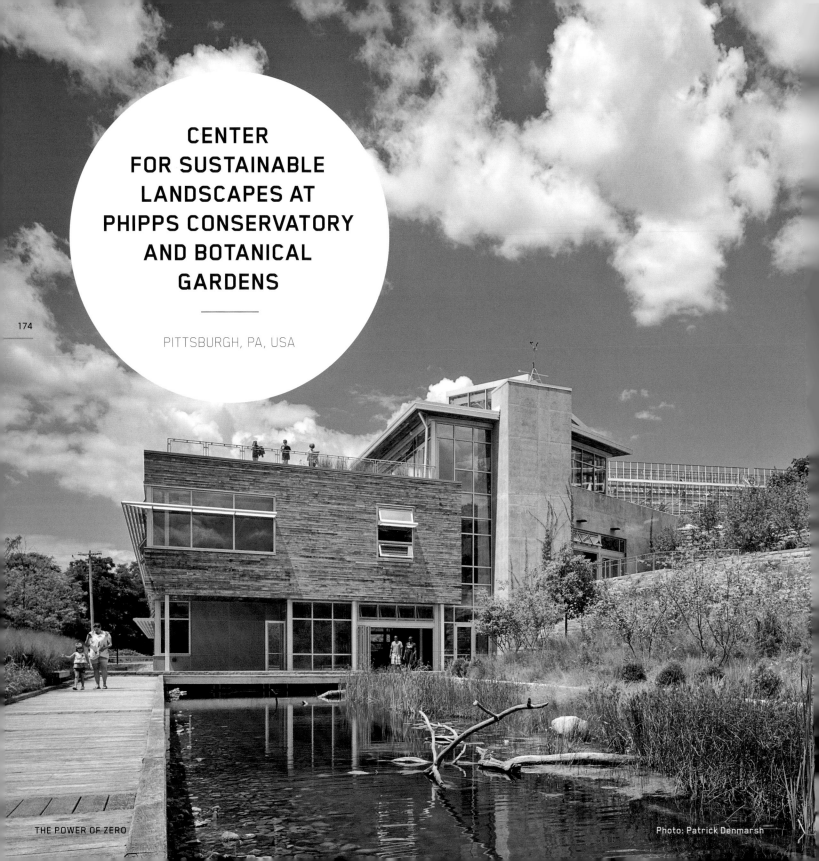

CENTER FOR SUSTAINABLE LANDSCAPES AT PHIPPS CONSERVATORY AND BOTANICAL GARDENS

PITTSBURGH, PA, USA

Photo: Patrick Denmarsh

PROJECT TEAM

OWNER: Phipps Conservatory and Botanical Gardens

ARCHITECT AND INTERIOR DESIGN: The Design Alliance Architects

CONTRACTOR: Turner Construction

STRUCTURAL ENGINEER: Atlantic Engineering Services

MECHANICAL, ELECTRICAL, PLUMBING: CJL Engineering

CIVIL AND GEOTECHNICAL ENGINEER: Civil & Environmental Consultants Inc. (CEC)

LIGHTING DESIGN: CJL Engineering

LANDSCAPE ARCHITECT: Andropogon

SPECIALTY CONSULTANTS: Evolve EA, HF Lenz, Indevco, Pitchford Diversified, 7group, Sundrive

SUBCONTRACTORS: Allegheny Installations, Allied Waste, Aquascape, Automated Logic, Berner International Corp., Brayman Construction, Tom Brown Contracting, Burns and Scalo, Compu-Site, Continental Building Systems, S.A. Comunale, Definis Mechanical Contractors, Dillion Well Drilling, D-M Products, Dubin and Company, Energy Independent Solutions, Engineered Products, Epiphany Solar Water Systems, A. Folino Construction, Franco, Franklin Interiors, Giffin Interior & Fixture, Glass House Renovation Services, Hanlon Electric, Lutron Electronics, Marshall Elevator, Massaro Industries, Mats Inc., A.G. Mauro, Mele Landscaping Contractors, Mendel Steel, Noralco Corporation, TD Patrinos Painting & Contracting, PPG Industries, Saints Painting, J.C. Schultz Interiors, SSM Industries, Spectra Contract Flooring, Tri-State Lockers & Shelving, Western Pennsylvania Geothermal Heating and Cooling

SIZE:
3 floors / 24,350 sf

BUILDING FOOTPRINT:
10,700 sf

SITE:
115,434 sf

TYPE:
Institutional

LIVING TRANSECT:
L3, Village or Campus Zone

WEBSITE:
phipps.conservatory.org/green-innovation/at-phipps/center-for-sustainable-landscapes

LOCATION:
Pittsburgh, PA, USA

EUI:
18.1 kBtu/sf/yr

PV SIZE:
125.25 kW (one ground and two roof mounted arrays)

OTHER RENEWABLES:
10kW vertical access wind turbine

CLIMATE ZONE:
Cold

ANNUAL ENERGY USE
ACTUAL:
129,876 kWh

SIMULATED/DESIGNED:
117,623 kWh

ENERGY GENERATED:
133,301 kWh

CERTIFICATION:
Full Living Building Challenge Certified; ILFI-certified Net Zero Energy Building

DATE CERTIFIED:
March 2015

175

The Center for Sustainable Landscapes (CSL) at Phipps Conservatory and Botanical Gardens is a profound expression of Living Buildings, uniting the Conservatory's mission with a level of environmental performance held by only a handful of buildings worldwide. In 1999, Phipps Conservatory launched the long journey of transforming their overall campus towards greater sustainability when its master planning began adjusting practices based on the nascent green building movement. The story of the CSL becoming a Living Building began in 2006, when the Phipps Conservatory Executive Director, Richard Piacentini, heard International Living Future Institute founder

Jason F. McLennan speak about the Living Building Challenge at the USGBC's GreenBuild conference. Richard was immediately taken with the vision of the Challenge, and within two months Phipps' board voted to pursue it for the CSL.

Today, the CSL is an expansion of a legacy Victorian era botanical conservatory and a signature Pittsburgh institution, uniting the Conservatory's historic mission of showcasing the beauty of plants with a new vision for the 21st century restorative humanity. With over

350,000 visitors a year, the CSL seeks to be a beacon of sustainability for Pittsburgh, engaging the community through education and inspiration.

Comprised of an office, classroom and research facility for Phipps, the CSL is built on a previously developed, remediated 2.6 acre brownfield owned by the City of Pittsburgh. A terraced outdoor garden greets visitors, highlighting plants indigenous to the climate and ecosystem of Pennsylvania through features including wetlands, tree groves and rain gardens hosting over 100 species

of plants. The three-story building has two consistently occupied floors, with a third atrium floor transitional space that serves as the main building entrance from the rest of the campus. The atrium is passively conditioned and has an interior greenhouse, while the remaining building area is fully conditioned with a mechanical system. The project has achieved full Living Building Challenge certification in addition to being LEED Platinum Certified, a pilot project for WELL Building Platinum level, and a Four Stars pilot project for the Sustainable SITES Initiative.

EUI: CENTER FOR SUSTAINABLE LANDSCAPES

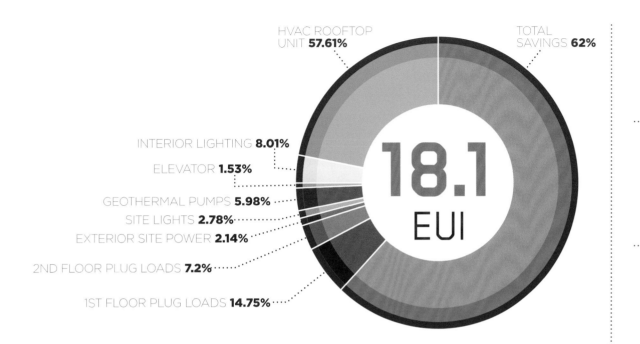

HVAC ROOFTOP UNIT **57.61%**

TOTAL SAVINGS **62%**

INTERIOR LIGHTING **8.01%**

ELEVATOR **1.53%**

GEOTHERMAL PUMPS **5.98%**

SITE LIGHTS **2.78%**

EXTERIOR SITE POWER **2.14%**

2ND FLOOR PLUG LOADS **7.2%**

1ST FLOOR PLUG LOADS **14.75%**

18.1 EUI

62%
SAVINGS FROM BASELINE

47.7
KBTU/SF/YEAR BASELINE EUI*

*ASHRAE 90.1 – 2007, Medium office category, all climates

CLIMATE AND SITE CONTEXT

The Center for Sustainable Landscapes is located in the Department of Energy's cold climate zone which typically has wide temperature ranges throughout the year. Temperatures of 5°F in the winter and 90°F in the summer are not unusual, placing significant energy demands on the heating and cooling system. Additionally, Pittsburgh can be humid during the summer, requiring the removal of humidity for efficient cooling (another energy demand).

FINANCING	
Soft costs:	$3,927,714
Hard costs:	$11,728,647
Price per square foot:	$643
Foundations/trusts:	$10,118,000
Individuals:	$3,160,070
Government grants:	$1,992,529
TOTAL PROJECT COST (excluding land purchase):	**$15,656,361**

ENERGY STORY: ACHIEVING NET ZERO AND BEYOND

Design process: The CSL involved a complicated design program which fit into a much larger, established institution with an array of operations, visiting public, research, and office functions. An extensive series of integrated design charrettes were held to ensure program functions were met, with a close eye to reducing energy demand wherever possible. The design team went through a series of design iterations looking at how low the energy use of the building could be reduced, with integrated reductions in lighting, heating, cooling, and user loads, ultimately settling on a target EUI of 19.2 kBtu/sf/year. In reality, the building performed at an EUI of 18.1 kBtu/sf/year, a testimony to the accuracy of the design team's work.

Passive first: An overarching design approach of the CSL was that wherever possible, passive systems that use little or no energy were employed. In a number of cases, baseline thermal needs were met using passive systems first, with mechanical systems only activated as needed—not unlike the DPR Phoenix project (page 88), which employed a similar strategy. A particularly interesting example of passive design in the building is the CSL atrium, which operates entirely without active heating and cooling. (The atrium and its highly innovative phase change material is discussed in more detail on page 180.)

This passive-first approach influenced the basic building layout, taking into account sun angle to maximize solar gain in the winter, minimize gain in the summer, and provide quality daylighting throughout the year. The resulting design is a wide and shallow structure running east/west.

DESIGN ELEMENTS

Envelope: Like almost all net zero energy buildings, the CSL has an excellent envelope. The wall structure is 2"x8" steel studs with water borne cellulose blown into the cavity. An additional layer of 2" rigid mineral wool was placed outside the sheathing, resulting in an overall R-value of R-25 to R-30. A rain screen system, with a skin of salvaged barnwood from southwestern Pennsylvania barns, was used for siding. On the roof, 8 inches of rigid insulation was used, with a green roof atop that, for a total R-value of R-42. Triple-paned low-e windows, appropriately tuned based on each aspect for appropriate solar gain, were used throughout the building.

Heating/Cooling/Daylighting/ Ventilation: The best net zero buildings integrate the systems and needs of the building seamlessly, making it difficult to categorize topically, as is the case with the CSL. The building takes a unified non-mechanical approach to provide a base of natural heating, cooling, daylighting, and fresh air within the building. On the south façade, interior/exterior light shelves prevent direct sun from entering the space during the summer, limiting solar gain while still bringing in daylight throughout the year. Deciduous trees were also placed to the south, which shade the building

during the summer, and diffuse strong daylight, while allowing the winter sun in. On the north façade, windows were also placed to provide ample ambient indirect daylight. Minimal windows are located on the east and west façades, given the difficulty in shading these aspects during the summer, and thus avoiding thermal gain. Computational fluid dynamic modeling was used to investigate air flows through open windows and optimize their placement. The result: windows on each floor positioned both high and low on the wall, allowing temperature mixing as air flows through the space.

The atrium is not mechanically heated or cooled, and relies entirely on winter solar gain and summer night cooling to maintain a reasonably comfortable temperature as a transitional space. A phase change material (see sidebar, page 180) was used which helps to stabilize temperature in the atrium in the 60-80 degree F range throughout the year. PEX tubing for a radiant hydronic heating system was installed as a safeguard if wintertime temperatures drop too low within the space. (Thus far, this has proved unnecessary.)

Although the CSL is able to rely on a significant amount of natural heating, cooling and ventilation, mechanical HVAC is also needed (given the demands of the climate). The centerpiece of this system is a ground source heat pump. A 14

UNDERFLOOR AIR DISTRIBUTION SYSTEM

Mechanically, the building is primarily served by an underfloor air distribution (UFAD) system. UFAD was selected because of its efficiency and low energy consumption relative to comparable systems. The UFAD provides optimum comfort control, while preventing over ventilation by reducing ventilation to unoccupied air volumes. Slow moving fans push air through the subfloor level, and up through vents in the floor. Ventilation air is introduced directly into the breathing zone, allowing heat from internal loads to stratify above the occupants. Air is then exhausted through ceiling vents. Overall, the system provides a substantial volume of fresh, clean air to the occupants of the building.

borehole ground source field is located under the driveway in front of the building. Because of limited area available, the boreholes and tubing are over 500 feet deep, providing adequate lineal exchange footage. (Typically, ground source boreholes must be placed at least 15-20 feet apart, or the ground is unable to adequately absorb the heating and cooling.) The pre-warmed/cooled fluid is then pumped to heat pumps which are located in a combined

PHASE CHANGE MATERIALS: DESIGN WITH NATURE

One of the most interesting phenomena in nature, called "phase change" by scientists, is the transition of materials from gas to liquid to solid, simply based on temperature. The poetry of melting ice, or disappearance of water as it evaporates, is one of the great simple pleasures of life—so basic and beautiful that it often does not even enter our conscious awareness.

One of the poetic elements of material phase change is that a great amount of energy is needed for a material to go through these transformations. One gram of liquid water requires one calorie of energy to change temperature by one degree Celsius—say from 50 to 51 degrees. But when that one gram of water is frozen, it requires 80 calories of energy just to melt, without any change in temperature, and for it to become steam (gas), it requires 540 calories. Similarly, for an ounce of steam to become water, 540 calories must be removed from it, and for water to freeze, 80 calories must be removed. This is why standing next to a waterfall is so enchanting—a lot of the liquid water becomes gaseous as it falls, and in the process it pulls energy out of the surroundings (including human bystanders) to do so. This principle is known as evaporative cooling.

A very innovative product, BioPCM, made by Phase Change Energy Solutions in North Carolina, uses the natural liquid/solid phase change of a proprietary soy-based product to retain and store heat and cold. Its phase change occurs at 73 degrees, an optimal temperature from the standpoint of thermal comfort. BioPCM is made as a sheet product, which can be fastened to the wall, flooring, or ceiling behind the finish surface. At the CSL, the material was placed in two areas: in the walls of the atrium for thermal massing, and in the drop ceiling in the office for nighttime cooling in the summer. During the summer, automated windows open at night to allow the cool night air (typically below 73 degrees)

into the atrium. The BioPCM—which is in a liquid state from the warmth of the previous day—hardens, and in the process of doing so, absorbs significant energy—far more than its weight would suggest. The following day, the BioPCM stays steadfastly at 73 degrees until later in the day, after enough heat energy has been absorbed, when it finally liquifies and begins its temperature rise once again. A similar process, but in reverse, occurs during winter when the significant southern glazing allows the atrium to rise above 73, and heat to be stored by the BioPCM which transitions to a liquid state, and then is released during the cold evenings. Overall, the BioPCM within the atrium acts as a flywheel, reducing temperature swings, and clipping highs and lows.

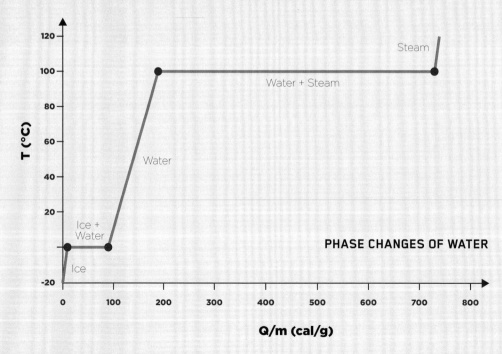

PHASE CHANGES OF WATER

rooftop unit made by Berner International Corp. headquartered in nearby Newcastle, PA.

The CSL's rooftop air handling unit features a filter module, air recirculation module, economizer, exhaust fan, enthalpy wheel for dehumidification, heat pumps, and compressors cooled by water. The unit is controlled by CO_2 and temperature monitors, and supplies 12,000 CFM.

Cooling of the Center for Sustainable Landscapes is facilitated in several modes. When outside air conditions permit, the building is cooled by natural ventilation through operable windows. This can be supplemented by a full economizing cycle on the rooftop unit. If necessary, the enthalpy wheel dehumidifier is activated, which removes excess humidity and reduces apparent heat without actually using heat pump based cooling. When temperatures are very high, the heat pump system is then activated to keep the space cool and comfortable. The CSL has a combination of automated mechanical and user controlled manual window opening and closing, based on the location and style of windows. Windows that are out of reach for occupants are controlled by the building's computerized building management system, which monitors temperature

and air quality. The lower windows are controlled by the occupants, giving them a sense of ownership and behavior engagements on the use of the building.

Lighting strategy: As discussed above, 80 percent of the needed light within the CSL is provided by daylight. Interior light shelves help light penetrate into the open space design which includes high cloud ceilings. Supplemental lighting includes high performance lighting equipment with daylighting sensors, controls, occupancy sensors, and dimming ballasts.

Renewables: Renewable energy is provided by a combination of solar and wind sources. (Notably, the CSL wind turbine is the only non-solar renewable energy used by any of the projects discussed in this book.)

To preserve the rooftop of the CSL for a green roof, the PV arrays needed to be located elsewhere, but still close enough to be connected and visibly associated with the Phipps campus. The 125.25 kW Solarworld photovoltaic system is divided into three arrays: one located on a building adjacent to the CSL, another mounted on the ground, and another roof mounted on the Special Events Hall. By virtue of proximity, any excess energy from the

solar array (not used by the CSL) is used by other buildings on-site, extending the renewable benefit of the system for the organization as a whole. The solar energy is converted to alternating current via a Sunny Boy inverter, which includes a web-based monitor accessible on-site, remotely and via smartphone, allowing user real-time feedback of the energy producing system.

The project also features a wind turbine located northeast of the CSL, which contributes to the overall renewable energy generation, and also serves as a visual and educational feature of what is possible with net zero energy design. The American-made turbine harvests wind from its vertically designed fans which are operable at lower wind speeds than typical turbines. It also is making it safer for birds and bats. The turbine is capable of generating up to 10,000 kWh a year, though during the NZE observation period at this location the system only generated 205 kWh, suggesting that its main value may be as an educational element.

Building management systems: Similar to the design of the windows, the automated system for controlling many of the building's functions incorporates occupant participation as part of its regulation. Building personnel are alerted to intervene when temperatures, humidity and ventilation levels might need to be shifted. It also lets building managers know when the outside temperature may be ideal for natural ventilation as opposed to mechanical.

Plug loads: Workstations include individual plug meters so workers can see their use in real-time. Six watt (6W) LED task lights are provided, along with smart power strips that disconnect the circuit once computers are shut down for the day. During "lunch and learns", occupants are engaged about how their at-desk energy use influences the net zero energy goals. Each month, plug load usage is reviewed as a group, and any issues with the space are discussed. This review highlights the benefit of net zero energy buildings that are entirely owner occupied: tighter coordination of achievement of the performance goal.

OCCUPANCY

The Phipps team found that commissioning and proper turnover was the key to getting the building running efficiently. This process took a full year's heating and cooling cycle to fully understand and evaluate the building. The team found a post-occupancy evaluation to be valuable, and revised significant parts of the HVAC and water management system programming based on it. The team has also found that metering feedback is critical to remain on target with NZE performance. Phipps is working with Carnegie Mellon University on original research related to building performance which has helped to improve operations and integrate user satisfaction. This research has enabled a reduction of EUI from 21 during the first year to the current EUI of 18.1. Based on submetering, Phipps was able to update the original energy model at the sub-use level, and create benchmarks to establish clear expectations about energy usage for all aspects of the building.

PAINTERS HALL

SALEM, OR, USA

PROJECT TEAM

OWNER:
Pringle Creek Community

ARCHITECT:
Opsis Architecture

GENERAL CONTRACTOR:
Spectra Construction

MECHANICAL ENGINEER:
Lyons Heating

ELECTRICAL ENGINEER:
Wallace First Choice Electric

STRUCTURAL ENGINEER:
DCI Engineers

PLUMBING:
3T Plumbing

SOLAR INSTALLER:
Tanner Creek Energy

ENERGY ANALYSIS:
Solarc

INTERIOR DESIGN:
Opsis Architecture

LIGHTING DESIGN:
Opsis Architecture

LANDSCAPE ARCHITECT:
Desantis Landscapes

SPECIALTY CONSULTANTS:
Wildwood Mahonia Native Plant Nursery, Barnwood Naturals, Taylor Metal, Evolution Paving, Cherry City Electric

The Pringle Creek Community outside of Salem, Oregon is a walkable neighborhood designed with integrated natural systems and a focus on building sustainably with the local ecology. Painters Hall, which resides at the center of the property, was built in the 1930s as a grain storage facility. (The hall was used by painters as an operations space in the 1950s and was thusly named). The original building was very well preserved, allowing the concrete foundation, walls, and wood trusses to be reused in the remodel, preserving the character of the space. Keeping with the aesthetic of the building, the hall's structure was retrofitted and redesigned into a high-performing, vibrant community center, cafe, gallery and meeting point for the Pringle Creek and Salem communities. The mixed-use building also features small office spaces and a kitchen. Visitors are greeted by a character-filled event space featuring reclaimed heavy timber, a salvaged steel trellis frame and a photovoltaic array. The building was renovated to USGBC LEED platinum standards and is a ILFI-certified Net Zero Energy Building. Construction began in April 2009 with the building occupancy starting a year later, in April 2010.

SIZE:
1 floor / 3,250 sf

SITE:
10,580 sf

TYPE:
Building - Office, Cafe, Assembly

LIVING TRANSECT:
L4. General Urban Zone

WEBSITE:
pringlecreek.com

LOCATION:
Salem, Oregon, USA

EUI:
20.83 kBtu/sf/yr

PV SIZE:
20.2 kW rooftop PV
of 96 Sanyo HIT 210N modules

OTHER RENEWABLES:
None

CLIMATE ZONE:
Marine

ANNUAL ENERGY USE:
ACTUAL: 19,845 kWh
SIMULATED/DESIGNED:
19,563 kWh

ANNUAL ELECTRICITY GENERATED:
2,297 kWh Excess Generation
(22,142 kWh)

CONSTRUCTION COST:
$192/sf

CERTIFICATION:
ILFI-certified Net Zero Energy Building

DATE CERTIFIED:
April 2012

186

ENERGY STORY: ACHIEVING NET ZERO AND BEYOND

Painters Hall is an excellent example of a historic retrofit that achieves the ultimate in energy performance. Another innovative aspect of the building is that it taps into a community-wide groundwater distribution system used for ground source heat pump prewarming. Energy produced by the Hall's photovoltaic array offsets requirements to operate pumps and associated systems.

FINANCING

Soft costs:	$39,922
Hard costs:	$412,102
Land:	$111,140
PV system design and installation:	$210,901
Public incentives (state, local, federal):	
Oregon business energy tax credit:	$81,154
Federal tax credit:	$47,235
Energy Trust of Oregon rebate:	$35,280
Private incentives:	None
TOTAL PROJECT COST (excluding land purchase & PV):	**$563,164**

EUI: PAINTERS HALL

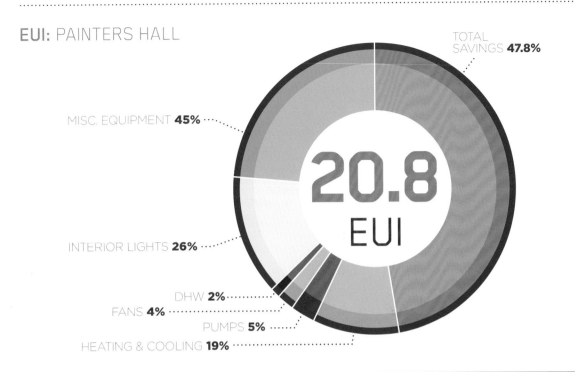

TOTAL SAVINGS **47.8%**

MISC. EQUIPMENT **45%**

INTERIOR LIGHTS **26%**

DHW **2%**

FANS **4%**

PUMPS **5%**

HEATING & COOLING **19%**

20.8 EUI

47.8%
SAVINGS FROM BASELINE

39.1
KBTU/SF/YEAR BASELINE EUI*

*ASHRAE 90.1 – 2007, Small office category, all climates

187

DESIGN ELEMENTS

Envelope: Similar to the Mission Zero Home, this retrofit significantly improved the thermal envelope. R-19 insulation was added to the building's existing eight-inch concrete walls and R-30 insulation was added to the attic floor. New double paned windows with a U factor of .30 replaced the originals. It is likely that the concrete walls and floor of the building provide a significantly better level of air sealing than a typical wood-framed building.

Heating and cooling: Painters Hall is part of the larger, very innovative Pringle Creek Community groundwater heat pump supply loop. Aligned with the focus of reducing its carbon footprint, the development repurposed a large existing irrigation well as an open-source ground source prewarming loop for a large part of the community. Rather than a more typical closed-loop system which requires a significant number of boreholes and network of piping, an open loop system relies on a single well, uses it for prewarming, and then reintroduces the water into the aquifer after use. Painters Hall receives a side feed from the Pringle Creek Community system and then uses a Water Furnace Envision water-to-air heat pump for heating and cooling the building. Air distribution within the building arrives via forced air ducts. Zonal electric heaters compensate the conditioning of the entire building when only a portion is occupied. The minor amounts of hot water needed are provided through point-of-use electric potable water heaters. Passive ventilation and cooling is provided through operable windows and a large 8' x 9' double door which connects indoor and outdoor spaces.

Natural daylighting: According to the design team and owners, Painters Hall is designed to function as a simple, open area space. The Hall can morph into many different configurations for multiple uses, a quality that lends to creativity and collaboration.

PART II: **NET ZERO PROJECTS**

Residents have developed their own programmatic uses unfettered by fixed walls, dedicated uses or obstructions. Overhead lighting is rarely used during the day as natural light enters the Hall from many windows and bounces off walls, ceiling, and flooring, which feels fresh and healthy. The aforementioned oversized double doors, when open, invite both natural light and fresh air into the building.

Renewable production: The PV array at Painters Hall generates electricity for the hall and its share of pumping energy for the neighborhood geothermal loop system, exceeding the modeled expectation and generating an excess of almost 23,000 kWh per year. The existing roof proved an excellent location for PV as it faces southwest and is also highly visible—providing a community icon of carbon neutral living. The panels have a tilt of 26 degrees and an azimuth of 205 degrees. The PV system is tracked by The Energy Detective monitoring system which records consumption, production and individual circuits for real-time awareness (which, in turn, encourages conservation practices). The renewable energy system is comprised of 96 Sanyo HIT 210N modules in four arrays which converts to alternating current via Advanced Energy PVP4800 string inverters.

EUI COMPARISON

The meta narrative that emerges from these wonderful buildings is very consistent: major improvements in energy efficiency are now possible using today's best design know-how and technologies. Moving civilization away from fossil fuels will require vast reductions in energy use, and we are already building functional prototypes.

Below, the Energy Use Intensities for the case study net zero energy projects are summarized (blue), relative to baseline energy use (shown in green). ASHRAE 90.1 – 2007, the required minimum for LEED projects, is used as the baseline for commercial and institutional buildings, while the 2009 Residential Energy Consumption Survey, administered by the US Energy Information Administration, was used for homes. The story told is a narrative of positive change towards a fossil fuel free future.

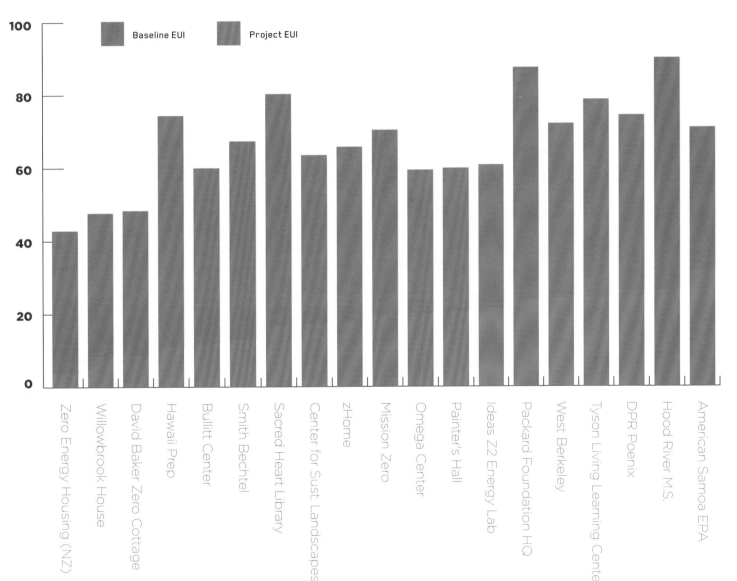

Legend: Baseline EUI / Project EUI

Projects (x-axis): Zero Energy Housing (NZ), Willowbrook House, David Baker Zero Cottage, Hawaii Prep, Bullitt Center, Smith Bechtel, Sacred Heart Library, Center for Sust. Landscapes, zHome, Mission Zero, Omega Center, Painter's Hall, Ideas Z2 Energy Lab, Packard Foundation HQ, West Berkeley, Tyson Living Learning Center, DPR Poenix, Hood River M.S., American Samoa EPA

NET ZERO ENERGY CHALLENGE

In 2014, the Institute began tracking the first certified Net Zero Energy Buildings across a range of building types and United States Department of Energy Climate Zones. The Institute challenges the community as a whole to grow, design, build, and occupy net zero energy buildings in every category, providing models across an array of sizes, occupancies, and geographies. As buildings are certified, they will be added to the Net Zero Energy Challenge Matrix.

	SINGLE FAMILY NEW	RETROFIT	MULTI-FAMILY
HOT HUMID		Willowbrook House	
MIXED HUMID	Zero Energy House		
HOT DRY			
MIXED DRY			
TEMPERATE	Eco-Sense Residence		zHome
COLD		Mission Zero House	
VERY COLD / SUB ARCTIC			

INTERNATIONAL LIVING
FUTURE INSTITUTE
www.living-future.org

THE POWER OF ZERO

LOW RISE OFFICE	MID & HIGH RISE OFFICE	EDUCATIONAL	INSTITUTIONAL	HEALTHCARE
		Hawaii Preparatory Academy	AS-EPA	
		Tyson Living Learning Center		
DPR Phoenix				
Integral Office				
Packard Foundation HQ	Bullitt Foundation	Bertschi School	Painters Hall	
		Omega Institute	Phipps Conservatory	

PART III

NET ZERO
COMMUNITIES

THE POWER OF ZERO

At the 2014 Living Future conference, the International Living Future Institute launched the Living Community Challenge (LCC), which takes the concepts of the Living Building Challenge to the neighborhood and community scale. Net positive energy is a key element of the LCC. While the LCC is still an emerging program, the Institute is quickly developing a framework of understanding for the issues and benefits of approaching net zero energy at the community scale. These are outlined below.

COMPLEXITY AND THE HUMAN FACTOR

Net zero and net positive energy communities necessarily bring with them a degree of complexity not found on individual building projects. Simply put, buildings are objects made up of systems; communities are systems composed of objects and people. This complexity inherent in communities allows them a degree of resiliency and sustainability that is not possible on the building scale alone. In nature, there are no sustainable or resilient objects; only systems are resilient. The strongest, most enduring, and most beautiful ecosystems are incredibly complex, with interrelations and symbiotic relationships that make the whole greater than the sum of the parts. The best communities also are characterized by the relationships and interdependencies that make their systems resilient. When viewed in this way, the appropriately leveraged complexity inherent in communities has the power to become their greatest strength. Net zero energy communities then may not be simply an alternative to net zero buildings, but the necessary evolutionary step in creating a regenerative future.

Chief among the complexities in operating on the community scale is people. While a building

> **"Net zero energy communities then may not be simply an alternative to net zero buildings, but the necessary evolutionary step in creating a regenerative future."**

may involve—usually at most—several owners and occupant groups, the best communities are quite diverse in terms of ownership and occupancy and may represent a wide variation in age, income, political opinion, religious affiliation, race, ethnicity, culture, and language. So, we ask: How can community organizers, planners, and government officials motivate a diverse group of people to organize around a common goal requiring sustained, coordinated action?

Other complexities involve the relationship of individual buildings to each other and to the community's net zero goals. Related to this goal are questions about energy distribution and storage, and to what extent these should be borne by public expense as traditional infrastructure or should be developed, owned, and maintained by the users. Finally, net zero energy communities quickly raise questions about mobility and access. Could a single-use bedroom community be net zero if all the residents rely on long, carbon-intensive commutes for work and other basic services?

Modern society is at a point in the trajectory of net zero energy as a concept that these questions about mobility and access do not have definitive answers—although these questions do serve as an important frame for the future. At the time of this book's publication there are few, if any, truly net zero communities around the world. However, there are a number of remarkably efficient and forward-thinking developments that are substantially powered by renewables and include net zero energy planning work which suggests a viable path forward. Below, lessons are derived from two existing communities—Hockerton in the United Kingdom and Vauban in the south of Germany—and from planning work for which the ILFI has been engaged with the city of San Francisco, the town of Normal, Illinois, and the District of Columbia's District Department of the Environment. These last three locations will also help to establish planning principles for the development of new and existing communities.

ISSUES AROUND NET ZERO COMMUNITIES

At present, net zero energy buildings tend to relate to one another in the same way that traditional buildings do in terms of resource sharing: typically, structures are isolated from each other. There are several ways in which sharing and the interrelationships within net zero energy communities have the potential to improve on the current model of grid-connected, but otherwise isolated, net zero energy buildings.

Thermal sharing is a core concept in the world of net zero energy communities. The basic idea of thermal sharing is that buildings which produce "waste" heat or cooling share that thermal asset with another building that can utilize the energy. This is particularly advantageous where buildings with dissimilar energy uses sit in proximity to one another. For example, industrial uses often generate a significant amount of excess heat as part of the manufacturing process. Similarly, computer servers generate significant heat as part of computing. At times, this heat can be a source of significant negative impact to the environment. (For example, heat discharged into local water bodies and into the air can raise overall temperatures, with negative consequences to fish and fauna.) As an alternative, excess heat can be shared with uses that need it. A classic, synergistic

THERMAL SHARING: SOUTHEAST FALSE CREEK ENERGY UTILITY

Nearly every building produces waste heat that is rarely utilized. Showers, sinks, dishwashers, washing machines, and even toilets (human waste is nearly 100 degrees) regularly dispose of low-grade thermal energy into the sewer system. The Southeast False Creek Energy Utility (SEU) in Vancouver, BC takes advantage of this dispersed waste heat generation by a technique called sewage heat recovery. The SEU system uses thermal exchangers in the sewer mains and heat pumps to turn this dispersed, low-grade heat source into a centralized, high-grade heat source which it shares via a thermal loop to a catchment area that is projected to include 7.4 million square feet of development on an 80 acre site (at full build-out). In this way, the SEU system essentially shares the waste heat of many users across the city with those in their service area through a district energy system. Individual buildings pull this thermal energy from the district system by use of energy transfer stations. These stations allow for a two-way, net-metered energy flow with the SEU, which adds another dimension to the thermal sharing capacity of the system. As of 2014, three buildings with solar thermal arrays were storing excess thermal energy in the SEU system. Through sewage heat recovery thermal net metering the SEU system is a pioneering example of thermal sharing through a district energy system.

District energy is perhaps the most commonly discussed shared resource possibility among those interested in planning, designing, and developing net zero energy communities. District energy may or may not involve thermal sharing. In its most basic form, it may simply involve a heating system with a single heat source distributed to multiple buildings. More sophisticated systems may involve thermal sharing, individual heating and cooling distribution loops, and generation of electricity in addition to heat (known as cogeneration).

District energy, like thermal sharing, is often spoken of in reverential tones as an ultimate solution, but it is only as good as the characteristics of the actual system. Planners, designers and developers must always delve into the details and evaluate the benefits of systems in creating a carbon-free world. Many, if not most, district energy systems use combustion-based boilers distributed through a network of pipes to individual buildings (which is really just an expanded version of a very typical CO_2 producing building heating system). At the individual building scale, such a system—especially if reinforced through binding legal agreements which require long-term participation—may actually serve to limit innovative approaches to reduce loads or generate carbon-free heating/cooling through use of heat pumps and renewables.

District energy systems are most compelling and powerful when they generate heating and cooling through highly efficient means and are powered by renewable sources. These networks share excess heating and cooling between buildings and uses without the use of combustion. Overall, district energy systems should be a tool for driving energy use per square foot lower than what would be otherwise be possible on a building-by-building level, or at a minimum to lower the per square foot cost on a building-by-building level.

Southeast False Creek, Vancouver, British Columbia. Image courtesy of Wikimedia Commons using Creative Commons 3.0

relationship exemplifying this point is industrial area waste heat being used to warm residential buildings.

Thermal sharing, however, is not always a panacea. The existence of excess thermal energy may be caused by inefficiency in the sharing use, rather than as an inherent aspect of the activity. In these cases, it is better to improve the efficiency of the system that is producing the waste, rather than institutionalize it by making other users reliant on its availability. Thermal sharing between buildings typically requires significant infrastructure and legal

frameworks, and if inefficiencies are hardened, we simply make it harder to unwind them. For example, within ILFI's work in Seattle's First Hill neighborhood, it was found that local hospitals produced significant waste heat—a finding that led to an investigation of potential thermal sharing. It was determined that the waste heat was derived from existing inefficient systems. Once these inefficiencies are addressed, waste heat will be reduced to an extent that it makes most sense to simply recapture the excess thermal energy within the hospitals themselves. The sharing of physical resources

and networks in the form of thermal energy and/or district energy is only one type of sharing made possible in net zero energy communities. There is a significant amount of inspiration, innovation, and action generated when a group of people work together towards a common cause. There is a long history of cities spurring innovation around a specific issue when a dedicated group of actors are inspired and empowered around a specific topic—like the birth of the skyscraper in 19th century Chicago, theatre on Broadway, finances on Wall Street, steel in 20th century Pittsburgh, technology

ALEXANDRA DISTRICT ENERGY UTILITY

In Richmond, British Columbia, the municipality developed a highly efficient ground source system which, at full buildout, serves 3.9 million square feet of mixed-use development in the Cambie neighborhood. The underground, closed-loop, ground source thermal exchange array is located in a community greenway. Heat pumps are located in a separate energy center building, with individual heat exchangers located in participating buildings. The system can provide either heating or cooling by running the system in reverse which helps to recharge the thermal resource. Because the system is a city-owned energy utility, all new construction within the district is required to connect through a service bylaw. This bylaw has ensured that Richmond's capital investment in the system is revenue positive. Additionally, this initiative has allowed development within the area to lower up-front costs by not requiring investment on a project-by-project basis.

At full buildout, it is projected that the system will reduce greenhouse gas emissions by 6,000 tonnes (about 6,614 tons) annually. The system is also designed to scale by allowing for connections to emerging technologies such as sewage heat recovery.

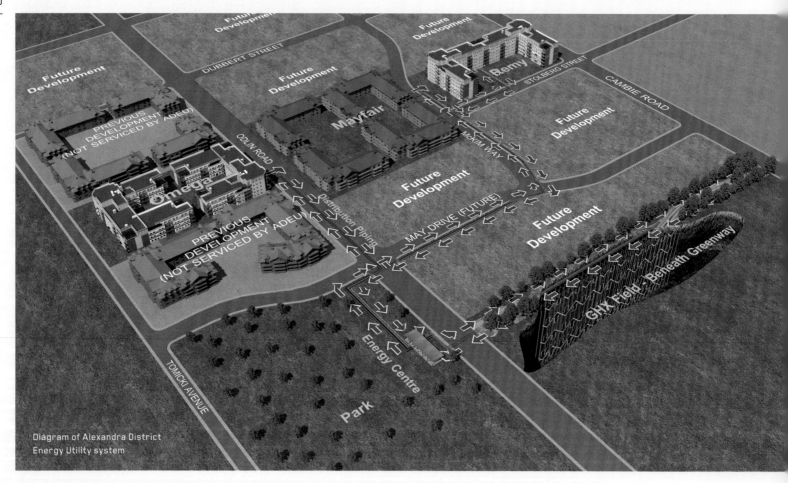

Diagram of Alexandra District
Energy Utility system

in Silicon Valley, automobile manufacturing in Detroit, higher learning in Oxford and Cambridge, foodie culture in Portland, and grunge music in 1990s Seattle. Similarly, the development of a net zero energy community opens up the potential of many people coming together to innovate and raise the bar around energy conservation and locally-based renewable energy generation, which can be very powerful indeed.

There is an example of this kind of energy spawning an innovation cluster in Issaquah, Washington. In the late 1990s, Issaquah was an early innovator in low toxicity materials and the use of structural insulated panels in the development of Pickering Barn, a legacy dairy farm repurposed as a community meeting and event space. Other projects followed. In 2003, the city completed Eastside Fire Station 72, the first LEED Silver certified building in the State of Washington. The Built Green Idea Home, developed by a public/private partnership in 2003, demonstrated interest in environmentally conscious building in the spec home market. After establishing a formal sustainable building policy in 2004, in 2006 the City led a coalition of partners to develop Net Zero Energy certified zHome [see page 38] as a culmination of knowledge and depth of performance. After the zHome development, the City also built the Maple Street Fire Station,

zHome, Issaquah, WA

> "Innovation clusters are a benefit and goal of net zero energy communities, although success is not guaranteed. There are certain risks present in developing net zero communities."

the world's most energy efficient fire station and recipient of the 2013 international ASHRAE Technology Award. Issaquah also led a residential weatherization and solarization campaign. Finally, Swedish Medical Center built a regional hospital in Issaquah with an extremely low EUI of 108 kBtu/sf (about one third of the national average). An array of leadership, know-how, inspiration and mutual influence led to an evolving level of performance within Issaquah. Issaquah's growing success provides a tangible lesson about the communal nature of innovation.

Innovation clusters are a benefit and goal of net zero energy communities, although success is not guaranteed. There are certain risks present in developing net zero communities. The tragedy of the commons (an idea borrowed from economics that was made popular in the 19th century) describes that with a commonly shared resource, individual actors are incentivized to minimize their contribution to that asset and maximize their extraction from it. This kind of behavior inevitably results in the asset's denigration and ultimate demise. This could be a concern for net zero energy communities in the sense that if regulatory agreements are not properly constructed, individual building operators could be motivated to pull more energy from the grid and not maximize efficiency so long as other buildings fill the delta. Recognizing this risk early on should allow planners and regulators to properly align incentives so that energy resources are accurately contributed, distributed, and utilized.

Another potential issue is the handling of peak loads. Traditional energy grids typically respond to peak loads by utilizing generators that can quickly fill the delta on demand, often with natural gas boilers. A community scaled system and grid based on renewable generation would obviously not have the luxury of fossil fuel powered, easily bootable generators. Battery storage provides one possible option for peak shaving, but may come with associated costs that are prohibitively expensive for some communities. Another option would be to collectively action to align behavior to match resource availability. Buildings themselves may be utilized as "batteries" when their use of energy corresponds with production. For example, maximizing heat pump operation during daylight hours (assuming photovoltaic production) may be a viable strategy. This approach would require a significant degree of community buy-in to the energy strategy not common in most energy planning.

Another beneficial element of community approaches to net zero energy is the ability to have dedicated programming, pooled purchasing, and other innovative ways to accelerate deep efficiency improvement on a broad scale. For example, the Green Impact Zone[1] in Kansas City, Missouri operated a program with a dedicated focus on improving the energy efficiency of a specific area of the city. This program improved energy efficiency in a particular study area through homeowner retrofit programs, and also provided training and employment opportunities to underemployed residents in the project area. This use of energy policy to accomplish both environmental and social justice goals simultaneously shows a possible powerful future for net zero energy community development and planning. Another example is the Seattle 2030 District where its dedicated group purchasing program for LED lighting reduces costs and facilitates the retrofit process for downtown businesses.

1   http://www.greenimpactzone.org/

202

LEGACY CASE STUDIES

At the time of the writing of this book the Living Community Challenge was only in its first year, and thus only a handful of communities had registered as part of the LCC, and no master plans had yet been developed. Below, a combination of existing, potentially net zero energy communities (not yet certified) and Living Community planning work done by the Institute provides examples and thinking about net zero energy communities.

HOCKERTON HOUSING PROJECT

The Hockerton Housing Project (HHP) is a collection of five attached single-family homes located in the rural village of Hockerton, Nottinghamshire, UK. Homes in the HHP are individually owned, but the solar resources are collectively owned, maintained, and utilized. This pioneering project was completed in 1998, and has evolved over time as a model of low carbon living, natural sewage treatment, sustainability education, and integration of beauty and community.

The building energy conservation strategy for the HHP is two-fold:

1/ Individual units of the HHP are essentially super insulated concrete boxes that include at least 300mm (nearly 1 foot) of concrete, 300mm of rigid foam insulation, and 400mm of earth. Due to the substantial mass of the concrete, there is some thermal regulation of stored energy on a short-cycle basis. Therefore, to achieve year-round passive thermal regulation, the project also relies on fully-glazed, south-facing conservatories along the length of each home. This allows the homes to use only solar gain for winter heating. Additionally, because the units rely heavily on a highly insulated, tightly sealed building envelope, the heat generated by household appliances and residents is a part of the thermal strategy. The orientation and design minimizes solar gain in the summer months while allowing natural ventilation for cooling. Average annual temperatures inside of the homes are reported to range from 17C (62.6F) in the winter to 24C (75.2F) in the summer months. The combined impact of these factors has allowed the HHP to operate using 10 percent of the energy required by a typical UK building, which translates to 8-11 kWh/day on average.

2/The second piece of the HHP energy strategy is community purchased, maintained, and utilized

Hockerton Housing Project, Nottinghamshire, UK
Photo: Brad Liljequist

renewables. These renewable are grid-connected and reportedly allow the community to achieve net zero energy on a net annual basis.[2] The HHP has two on-site wind turbines and two PV arrays that together can generate 24.65kW of peak power. An initial PV array and wind turbine were installed early in the project with a second PV array and turbine added later to help bump the project into a use/production balance. The use of diverse renewables has meant that 50 percent of the electricity generated is used on-site, with the other half exported to the grid. The renewable resources are collectively owned and their benefits are collectively realized, which has proven an effective strategy in keeping building energy consumption low.

An interesting sidenote to the HHP is the Sustainable Hockerton community group. Based on the leadership of the HHP, a group of villagers—including all of the HHP residents—collectively purchased a commercial-grade wind turbine that offsets the energy of 54 Hockerton village homes. This effort is exemplary of how a small community can spur larger, town-wide change. Additionally, this added generation potential is more than sufficient to offset the energy used at the HHP community and coworking space, Sustainable Resource Centre.[3]

2   Technical Factsheet: Energy Generation (Part 2).
Hockerton Housing Project Trading LTD, 2014.

3   Phone interview with Simon Tilley, Hockerton Housing Project Director. Interview conducted by Adam Amrhein on 15-06-19.

CASE STUDY:
THE VAUBAN NEIGHBORHOOD

Vauban is a neighborhood in Freiburg, Germany—a city that has been a leader in the country's environmental movement for sometime, starting with the rejection of a nuclear power plant proposed in the region in the 1970s. Currently, the green economy is a backbone of the city's economic portfolio, including 12,000 workers and 2,000 firms working in the environmental sector. Among these firms is Fraunhofer, the leading solar research institute in Europe. Freiburg has a goal to be powered 100 percent by renewable energy by 2050. Given these factors, the Vauban neighborhood's focus on renewable energy is exemplary.

Vauban is located on the former site of a post-World War II French military base southwest of the city center. The 40 hectare site is primarily residential, and includes 5,000 plus inhabitants and 2,000 residences. Green building is mandated on the site by requiring all new construction to achieve 65 kWh/m2, which translates to an EUI of 20.6. In practice, the building-by-building strategy to meet this strict standard has taken a variety of forms. In every case, however, building efficiency, renewable energy, and combined heat and power are the basis of the community's energy strategy.

Of particular interest to the topic of net zero energy communities are the Sonnenschiff (Solar Ship) and Solarsiedlung (Solar Settlement), designed by Rolf Disch. These buildings are all designed to Passivhaus standards, which include super-insulated building envelopes and orientation to maximize solar gain in the winter. The Sonnenschiff building is mixed use. Underneath the Sonnenschiff are two levels of parking and storage. The main massing of the building includes ground floor commercial space with office space above, and nine 3-story townhouses located on its roof. Immediately adjacent to the Sonnenschiff is the

"Vauban is a neighborhood in Freiburg, Germany — a city that's been a leader in the country's environmental movement for sometime, starting with the rejection of a nuclear power plant proposed in the region in the 1970s. Currently, the green economy is a backbone of the city's economic portfolio, including 12,000 workers and 2,000 firms working in the environmental sector."

Solarsiedlung, which includes 50 townhouse units. These efficiently designed buildings, combined with good solar orientation and maximum rooftop cover of PV units, make the Sonnenschiff and the Solarsiedlung examples of Plusenergiehaus buildings which, according to the architect, means that they generate more electrical energy than they consume annually. (It should be noted, however, that the buildings in both the Sonnenschiff and Solarsiedlung connect to the district CHP system for heating, which relies on combustion for energy generation. Yet, in both cases, the buildings reportedly generate enough energy through their PV arrays to offset the thermal energy provided by the CHP.)

In addition to building efficiency and energy generation strategies, the Solarsiedlung and Sonnenschiff in particular, and the Vauban neighborhood generally, have achieved a transportation strategy that drastically reduces motor vehicle use; 70 percent of residents within Vauban are reportedly car-free. This is made possible by the provision for ample public transportation, limiting parking to two consolidated garages on the north end of the site and along the commercial core, and by flipping the street paradigm to favor pedestrians and cyclists rather than automobiles. Not only has this strategy allowed for a drastic reduction in transportation energy, it has allowed for the street infrastructure to be more multi-functional. The transit right-of-way (ROW) doubles as a stormwater swale and the residential streets are known as play-streets, providing a significant open space amenity to residents.

Views of Vauban, Germany. Images courtesy of www.vauban.de, liscensed under Creative Commons Attribution 3.0

Charrette with Green
Alleys neighborhood
group in Noe Valley, CA

PLANNING FOR NET ZERO ENERGY COMMUNITIES

The International Living Future Institute has engaged in high-level planning with the introduction of the Living Community Challenge (LCC). Though these efforts have been focused on the LCC generally, they include a dedicated focus on net zero energy. Two of the three planning efforts discussed below are in largely built-out existing areas, which introduces additional issues into the concept of net zero energy communities. In existing communities many more people are involved, and typically there is no central authority to mandate performance levels. Existing buildings are generally only cost effective to retrofit in conjunction with a larger deep remodel, making the pace of improvement very slow. However, as we seek to limit our human footprint, improving and evolving existing communities is imperative. The following details some challenges faced, lessons learned, and possibilities in planning for net zero energy communities.

Rendering of blue-green
street in Noe Valley, CA

STUDY AREA:
NOE VALLEY, SAN FRANCISCO, CALIFORNIA, UNITED STATES

The ILFI project team was engaged in this particular study area as a part of a larger planning process with the City of San Francisco on neighborhood planning for sustainability. A seven block portion of the Noe Valley neighborhood was selected based on the existence of, and interest by, a community group championing green alleys in their neighborhood.

As discussions evolved to focus on energy use, one simple question arose: *Can a typical residential area in San Francisco achieve net zero energy, and if so, what would it take?*

Noe Valley is located near the center of San Francisco, and is bordered by the Mission District, the Haight, and the Twin Peaks neighborhoods. The study area includes primarily residential uses along with a few commercial and institutional buildings. The residences are row-houses—

many of which have been subdivided into several units, medium density apartment buildings of no more than four stories, and alley houses on subdivided lots. The assessment of net zero energy potential in the study was in three parts: current use, optimal future use, and potential renewable energy production.

Current energy use estimates were based on a manual count of the housing units within the study area, average household size information from the 2010 U.S. Census, and existing City energy use data for residents per capita. While this latter information is based on observation and well vetted data sources, it relied on aggregated averages and generalizations. More detailed current energy use information could be attained through individual utility account information, but that was outside of the scope of the project.

With the baseline energy use projection in place, the project team worked to establish an optimized energy use goal for the study area. (Note: This is a crucial step working in existing places.) Given the generation potential of current renewable energy technologies, net zero energy within the boundaries of the community is only possible when paired with deep energy conservation and building efficiency. Since the study area in Noe Valley is largely built out, save for a few institutional surface parking lots which might be redeveloped, the project team assumed that the bulk of building efficiency retrofits would happen over time as individual buildings undergo significant renovations. In practice, this would be a long-term strategy that would need to be supported by dedicated programming and clear guidelines and resources made available to the building owners prior to the start of improvements. To establish the optimized energy use in the study area, the project team used regional Living Building Challenge and NZE certified projects of comparable building types and uses. With these as the benchmark, the project team assumed that the study area could achieve a 57 percent reduction over current energy use.

Solar generation potential for the study area was derived from the roof area multiplied by a useable area factor, average solar exposure at that latitude, and the average generation efficiency of current solar panels. The useable area factor was determined by the project team, applying best judgement based on roof angles, parapets, etcetera. Solar exposure and generation efficiency was based on the online PV Watts program, operated by the U.S. National Renewable Energy Laboratory. The project team assumed that the study area would remain grid connected, pulling energy from the grid when the panels were generating less than needed, and pushing excess energy back into the grid.

Study Area in Noe Valley, CA

Original Uptown Normal plan area with now iconic traffic circle.

209

Using this methodology, the project team found that the Noe Valley study area could generate 140 percent of the community's building energy needs on a net annual basis. Additionally, given that the goal to bring the neighborhood to net zero energy is a long-term strategy, it is entirely possible that the generation potential will increase over time as panels become more efficient. Furthermore, the project team only considered roof area for PV panel siting; including portions of the ROW or surface parked sites would add to the solar generation potential.

Building energy use is only part of the planning needed to achieve community carbon neutrality; the next most significant consideration is transportation. In Noe Valley, the project team worked with City staff and local community members to charrette some ideas related to the street and alley infrastructure in the study area. The result was a network of streets and alleys with enhanced bicycle and pedestrian access and decreased automobile access. This network, combined with a community car share program, could drastically reduce transportation energy use. Additionally, if the community car shares were electric vehicles they could act as a battery to store the excess electrical energy, thus closing the loop on net zero energy buildings, energy storage, and net zero energy transportation.

STUDY AREA:
SOUTH UPTOWN, NORMAL, ILLINOIS, UNITED STATES

The South Uptown neighborhood of Normal, Illinois is well-known amongst the green design and development community as an early LEED for Neighborhood Development (LEED-ND) project. Normal was also the first small city to require LEED certification for new buildings over a certain size. The original planning and design work for the redevelopment of Uptown was executed by Farr Associates of Chicago in the early 2000s. The redevelopment of Uptown has largely been successful, with many elements of the original plan now realized. In 2014, Normal began planning

Aerial view of Normal, IL.

NORMAL CARRYING CAPACITY: ENERGY

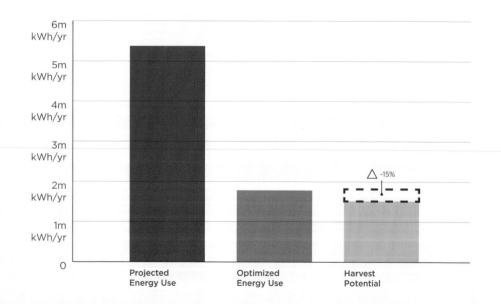

for the redevelopment of a 7-acre municipally owned parcel immediately south of Uptown, and registered the area as the second Living Community Challenge project. The ILFI was brought in by Farr Associates to assess the feasibility of the project achieving Living Community Challenge certification. Though the project was still in the planning phase at the time of this book's publication, lessons for planning for net zero energy communities may be derived. The first and perhaps most important lesson learned thus far is to begin planning for net zero energy early in a project's development. Because net zero energy was a consideration for the project by the client team early in the planning process, they had opportunity to adjust density, use, orientation, and form to meet that goal. Additionally, early planning allows efficiency and system design standards to be included in the regulatory structure of the site. Short of building a completely net zero energy community in one step, new construction could be required to be solar-ready and have efficiencies that will allow for on-site net zero energy generation. Planning for net zero so early in the process will also allow the project team more options for generation and improved efficiency through thermal sharing or ground source wells. The opportunity to include the ROW, open spaces, and area under the buildings as a part of the strategy is an option that many existing communities do not have.

The ILFI analysis of net zero energy potential revealed that at Living Building Challenge levels of efficiency (that is, an average EUI of 20), the planned development program for South Uptown could generate 85 percent of the project's building energy needs using rooftop solar generation alone. In addition to the strategies mentioned above, to achieve net zero energy a carefully planned and thoughtfully executed scale jump is available to the project. Given the project's location, wind energy is a viable option. In fact, there are already wind generation resources being developed within view of Normal, such as at Heartland Community College and High Trail Wind Farm. Both of these sources would be viable options to close the energy generation gap on the project.

STUDY AREA:
DISTRICT OF COLUMBIA, UNITED STATES

In 2012 the District of Columbia released its 20-year Sustainable DC plan. In it, Mayor Vincent Gray announced the goal to transform DC into "the greenest, healthiest, and most liveable city in the United States." It includes goals such as: cutting energy use by 50 percent citywide; increasing the share of energy provided by renewables to

50 percent; cutting greenhouse gas emissions by 50 percent; and making 75 percent of all trips by walking, biking, or public transit. Many cities with such an aggressive framework in place would simply work towards their goals and evaluate success and next steps at the end of the planning horizon. To the District's credit, the forward-thinking leaders in the District Department of the Environment (DDOE) have recognized that, while the Sustainable DC Plan is an important tool and worthwhile vision, it is not ultimately the City's end game. After all, a city that is 50 percent powered by renewable energy is still 50 percent powered by non-renewable energy, and a city that has reduced greenhouse

gas emissions still has greenhouse gas emissions, and so forth.

In 2015, DDOE convened a working group of 40 public and private sector leaders to envision DC's sustainability endgame. The ILFI was asked to work with DDOE on goal setting and facilitation of the charrette. In preparation of this work, the ILFI project team prepared a similar energy use/harvest analysis as described in the above sections.

The working group agreed that by 2050, DC should be powered 100 percent by locally generated, renewable energy. Based on the ILFI analysis, this would mean that approximately 16,500 GWh/yr would

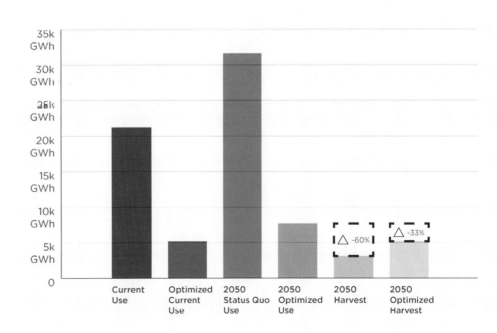

WASHINGTON DC CARRYING CAPACITY: **ENERGY**

212

Could DC's water collection weir on the Potomac River be rebuilt as a run-of-the-river hydro source? Photo courtesy of esm.versar.com

need to be generated using renewable energy, assuming business-as-usual development sufficient to capture projected population growth. If the city also enacted an aggressive efficiency and conservation strategy for new building and deep retrofits, the ILFI team found that energy use could be not only more than halved, but be lowered well below the current energy use of 11,000 GWh/yr. Using regional precedents, it could be possible to reduce 2050 energy use in DC by 63 percent to 7,690 GWh/yr.

There had been several assessments of the District's solar generation

potential prior to the ILFI analysis, including those by GDS Associates, the National Renewable Energy Laboratory, and Mapdwell. The ILFI analysis differed from these in that it assumed an increase in panel efficiency by 2050 within the physical limitations of current technology. It also assumed an increase in roof area and roof area optimization for solar as the city becomes more dense to accommodate projected residential growth. The ILFI analysis found that by 2050, the rooftop solar generation potential for the District could be 5,170 GWh/yr. This means that by 2050 the District could source 67

percent of its energy using only rooftop solar generation, which amounts to approximately 14 percent of the total land area in the District.

To close this 33 percent delta, there are many options available to the district that take advantage of some portion of the remaining 86 percent of its land. Options discussed at the

The DC tidal basin releases half a billion gallons of water every day: could it be converted into a tidal renewable system?
Photo: Ron Cogswell / Flickr Creative Commons

working group meeting in March 2015, included expanded sewage heat recovery for added efficiency, utilizing parts of the ROWs for solar trellises, run-of-river hydroelectric generation, the utilization of DC's tidal basin, wind either on or off of the rivers, biogas recovery, and regionally dispersed solar. If this last option was applied, the project team found that approximately 6 square miles of land would be required (about 9 percent of DC's land area).

Any very large scale plan to transition to renewable energy necessarily brings with it questions and considerations about energy storage and distribution. This is to say that a renewably powered future based on distributed generation implies a different function and role for energy utilities and perhaps a new way that users interact with, and relate to, electrical energy consumption. These considerations, and several others, will be developed in the following chapter.

PART IV

A NET POSITIVE FUTURE

Net Zero Energy — the first stage in a transformation toward a carbon free future.

Net zero energy buildings, as compelling and meaningful as they are, are just a beginning. We are only in the earliest days of a revolution in net zero energy design and technology. The energy use intensity of net zero energy buildings will continue to drop, the efficiency and output of their renewables will increase, and the cost of the whole package will come down, making net zero energy projects more common. New design ideas and technologies will evolve, enabling new pathways for achieving this vital concept.

It is critical to understand, however, that net zero energy buildings, and even net zero energy communities, do not get us where we need to be if our end goal is the total elimination of fossil fuel usage. Net zero enegy buildings are not a universal solution — they are just a component. For us to achieve total elimination of fossil fuels, a deeply integrated revolution in buildings, mobility in terms of transportation, and the power grid must occur.

So what advancements are on the horizon?

David & Lucile Packard Foundation Headquarters, Los Altos, CA

343 Second Street

NET ZERO ENERGY BUILDING DESIGN AND TECHNOLOGIES — THE NEXT GENERATION

The boundaries of passive and active systems blur

As knowledge of net zero design builds, the notion of an approach being "passive" or "active" is beginning to fade. Net zero energy buildings are partially built on the heritage of passive solar buildings of the 1970s, which at least from a heating and cooling standpoint relied on simple thermal gain and storage. As the net zero revolution began, a heavy reliance on sophisticated technologies — heat pumps and LED lighting being primary examples — dominated the discussion. Today, however, the best NZE buildings seamlessly combine both passive and active design concepts and, in fact, it is becoming increasingly difficult to describe them in those terms. For example, the Bullitt Center utilizes a highly sophisticated software program using real time weather data to open and close windows depending on wind direction, providing natural cooling and ventilation when needed. Those same windows also allow passive solar gain, but only during cooler months, and only if the computerized system opens the exterior shades. The passive solar gain typically contributes only a part of the needed heat which is also provided by the heat pump system. Are these systems active or passive?

Mostly, they are just thoughtfully designed with an attention to naturally occuring assets. Moving into the future, sensitively designed systems which take maximum advantage of nature's gifts will become the norm.

Micro heat pumps

The revolution in heat pumps will continue, with a new focus on micro systems, which allow appropriate load matching for low heating/cooling demand buildings with excellent thermal envelopes. Recently, Sanden, a major automobile heat pump/air conditioner manufacturer, entered the building market, thereby suggesting new movement in this area.

Elimination of high GWP compression gases from heat pumps

Today, high global warming potential compression gases, such as HFC's, are used in heat pumps. These substances have the potential to leak, creating an additional impact on the climate. The shift from combustion to heat pump based heating systems must be accompanied by a shift to CO_2 as the primary compression gas for heat pumps, lest we simply replace one problem gas for another. Thankfully, this shift away from global warming compression gases is beginning to occur.

High performance windows become the norm

Today windows typically used in net zero energy buildings, with U-values in the 0.20's, are fairly custom, with high price tags. However, as glazing and window technology matures, and especially as jurisdictions begin to codify lower U-values for the purpose of energy management, these windows will become much more prevalent, similar to the switchover to low-E glass that happened a decade ago.

Dedicated focus on high energy use sectors

Certain very high EUI building types — hospitals, restaurants, factories, data centers, and supermarkets in particular — lag in innovation relative to other sectors. These buildings use vastly more energy per square foot than primary buildings like homes and offices. The energy modeling for one potential net zero energy building found that a high volume coffee shop storefront would have an equivalent energy footprint to the offices in the rest of the building — which had twenty times more square footage. While these EUI building types inherently have high demands, there is ample room for innovation. For example, many medical devices have not undergone the same efficiency transformation that has rippled through the appliance market. Also, it is still common design practice in supermarkets to exhaust

Mitie Group Data Center
Photo: Ed Robinson/OneRedEye,
Flickr Creative Commons

heat from refrigerators to outdoors, instead of using it resourcefully for internal heating. In restaurants, an ethos often exists of running stoves at 100 percent despite the actual need, and the heat pump revolution has yet to arrive to kitchen hot water equipment. Technologies such as CO_2 heat pumps, which produce much higher temperature water than conventional heat pumps, suggest that new approaches are on the horizon.

Revolution in retrofit technologies

Shy of a complete building overhaul, today it can be challenging to deeply retrofit a building for very low energy use. However, here too, strides are being made to facilitate the retrofit process and reduce the cost. Thermal imaging cameras, a critical tool in understanding building heat and cold leakage, have become radically cheaper, and soon should become a standard toolbox item. Heat recovery ventilators, long an obscure, rarely seen item, are now available in the hundreds, rather than thousands of dollars. Perhaps most exciting is the introduction of vacuum insulation panels from manufacturers such as Panasonic, that offer extremely high R-values per inch.

Revolution in building mounted renewables

The cost of solar panels has been dropping significantly, suggesting a maturing of the technology and, as panel costs decrease and solar technology becomes more commonplace, other elements of solar installation are being focused on. Better integration of solar applications during the design process, particularly to facilitate mounting, will bring solar costs down even further. At the same time, panel efficiency marches ever upward — 15 percent was typical just several years ago, but 20 percent is now available in the marketplace, while 40 percent has been achieved in laboratory conditions. While these performance improvements conveyed as a percentage may seem small in terms of marginal improvement from baseline, improvements average about 5 percent per year, which is quite significant over time.

And yet, a much deeper revolution in solar generation is brewing with thin film, omnidirectional solar cells. Ideally these will absorb sun energy with less regard for solar angle, and will be able to be installed as

Tesla Powerwall
Photo: Alexis Georgeson, courtesy of Tesla

a wrapped skin, perhaps in lieu of paint. This technology will transform building energy generation again, with potentially much higher levels of building production because panels can be placed in a much broader array of locations, including walls.

Revolution in energy storage

Finally, there is the brewing revolution in electrical storage led by Tesla and the automotive sector. This technology brings us back to the roots of net zero buildings — the off-the-grid passive buildings of the 1970s. A potential end game of this technology could be a significant decrease of the conventional grid as individual buildings become more autonomous in their use and production of energy.

THE END GAME

The discussion of the energy end game leads us to the right final question — ideally, what should a fossil fuel free, entirely renewable energy future look like? What is the end game? And what are its characteristics?

The current divestment movement suggests a beginning to a future independent of fossil fuels. The activist pioneers are simply saying "no" — withdrawing from the fossil fuel world entirely, in this case with their dollars. As we say "yes" to a new energy future, we must also say "no" to negative systems. The truth is that net zero energy buildings, as revolutionary as

they are, still are predicated on an electrical grid that is largely based on fossil fuels. Similarly, our mobility is predominantly powered by fossil fuels as well. For the revolution to be complete, the energy grid and transportation must be transformed just as radically as buildings. Fossil fuels must be eradicated in their entirety, replaced by renewables, everywhere, within the grid and mobility alike.

So what might that look like?

All renewable electrical grid

The reality of renewably generated electricity being less expensive to produce is now becoming reality in many parts of the world. While conservation is still cheaper, the basic financial fundamentals associated

THE DUCK CURVE
NET LOAD- MARCH 31

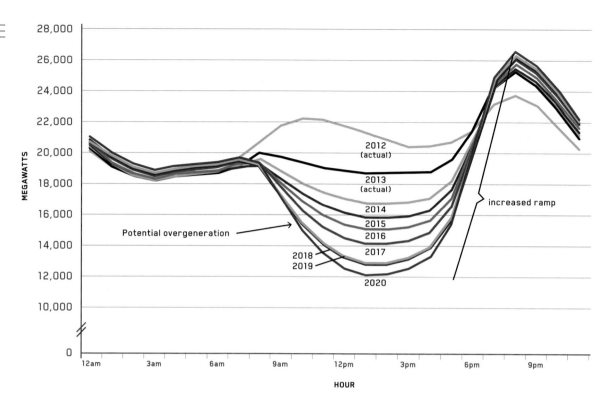

with renewably generated technology have reached a tipping point, which the market is beginning to awaken to. As it becomes cheaper to produce electricity using renewables than with fossil fuel power plants, the shift will be complete, as the free market will do the transformative change on its own. The question then turns to how a 100 percent renewable system might work, since the renewables of sun and wind cannot run 24/7, given that they are based on nature's activity rather than on our own demands. Over time, net zero and low EUI buildings and the power grid must co-evolve to match each other's constraints and needs.

The often mentioned, frequently misinterpreted "duck curve" suggests how this evolution might occur. While the duck curve is specific to California, it is similar to other places in the world, and generally suggests that each grid location has its own constraints and use profile.

The duck curve is simply a projection of what the energy load might look like as renewables become more prevalent. Currently, loads vary throughout the day, but with some consistency. Renewable production, which of course peaks in the middle of the day, could make things difficult for utilities by creating a large

swing in daily demands on the grid, because net zero buildings would need little grid energy during the day (since they are making their own power) but they would still need to pull energy off the grid at night.

The truth is, however, that net zero energy buildings can be easily designed to use power at their time of peak energy production. A benefit of highly efficient building envelopes is that they retain cold and heat for longer periods of time. Natural nighttime cooling can be held throughout the day. Similarly, heating systems which typically might be turned on at night can run during the day, when the sun is out. A net zero building that is well designed to use power when it is produced, with a small amount of storage for the few uses that must happen during dark periods, such as lighting and entertainment systems, will have little demand on the grid.

This revolution in micro grids and battery storage, led by SolarCity and others, completes the picture. Buildings will begin to store energy in batteries, and in so doing become nearly grid independent – indeed, many buildings will go fully off the grid. But the benefits of energy sharing, and the core fact that utility scale renewables are much cheaper than building mounted renewables, will mean that the grid is likely to continue to exist. The grid itself can also take advantage of very large scale, chemical free electrical storage, and does so already for peaking demands. Today, California has substantial pumped hydro storage, which stores electricity by pumping water with a reversible turbine from a lower to an upper reservoir, and running it back to the lower reservoir when power generation is needed. Pumped hydro storage, and thoughtful integration of appropriate hydro power, can help balance grid demands in general.

Mobility revolution

As buildings and industry become more efficient, mobility

"While conservation is still cheaper, the basic financial fundamentals associated with renewably generated technology have reached a tipping point, which the market is beginning to awaken to."

221

Zero Cottage,
San Francisco, CA

must become right sized, and either human or renewably powered.

As the era of fossil fuels must end, so too must end the era of very large, disproportionately sized personal mobility devices. In 2009, the average vehicle occupancy in the United States for home/work trips was 1.13 people per car, and the average vehicle weight was about 4,000 pounds. This means we are using 4,000 pounds to transport about 200 pounds of people. In the meantime, the large size of vehicles takes up space on the roads leading to gridlock. Smaller scaled, small footprint vehicles, such as the two seat electric Renault Twizy, with an MPG equivalent of 211, will join walking, bicycling, and transit in a paradigm shift in transportation, which matches the mobility tool with the actual demand. The ramifications of this transformation for our cities, which average about 30 percent of their area as vehicle right of way, are enormous. Automobiles, which now dominate the cityscape, can give way to beauty, rewilding, human scaled mobility corridors, blue green streets, and green infrastructure as lane widths diminish.

Long distance travel perhaps is the greatest challenge in a fossil fuel free future, but even here solutions exist. High speed, electrified rail has transformed mobility in many countries. The mechanical efficiency of steel wheel train travel is extremely high, with an effective efficiency of five to twenty times higher than automobile or jet travel per passenger mile. Finally, the biofuel revolution in jet fuel suggests a path forward even in that arena. It is possible that the end game of our culture overall will be entirely focused on electrification, with biofuels used only for their highest and best use, where extremely high energy:weight densities are needed, such as in aeronautics.

Renault Twizy
Photo: David Kirsch,
Flickr Creative Commons

California bullet trains
Photo: California High Speed Rail Authority

223

Center for Sustainable Landscapes at
Phipps Conservatory and Botanical Gardens,
Pittsburgh, PA

CONCLUSION

We are, of course, a long way from that future. The change to this sustainable future is exacerbated by the fact that this challenge is fairly different than those of the past. Hair trigger mechanisms embedded deep in our DNA, those of fighting enemies and other immediate emergencies, are not triggered by this longer term, intergenerational crisis. And those impacted are the least able to respond.

But the story of human history has been one of challenge and response. This is the story of our time. Together we can respond and grow. Perhaps it is time for us, as humans, to evolve a new sense of what it means to be homo sapiens — to be stewards of each other and the planet — what Jason F. McLennan has coined "Homo Regenesis". If the last ten years has been any indication, we do have the means at hand to evolve past

fossil fuel use. A decade ago, when focus began to be placed on carbon neutral buildings, they seemed like a very far off reality — but we already have entered an era of second generation net zero buildings. It now appears realistic that the complete transformation to a fossil fuel free culture can occur within our lifetime.

As mentioned above, the key tipping point in the transformation of energy production and use is the evolving change in costs which make renewable energy less expensive than new fossil fuel based generation. This change will simply become more prevalent over time, as a compelling technical, environmental, and financial case for renewable and efficient living solidifies, and ultimately, the fossil fuel era will come to an end. The momentum is terrific. Working together, building off each other in a broader community, we can make the change.

225

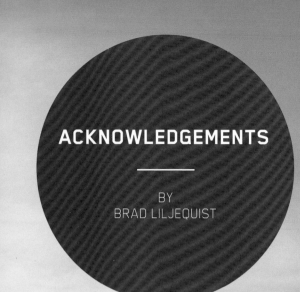

ACKNOWLEDGEMENTS

BY
BRAD LILJEQUIST

Omega Center for Sustainable Living, Rhinebeck, NY

The creation of this book was made possible through a generous grant from the Packard Foundation, a strong defender of the planet and people for many years. The Foundation has been a powerful champion in creating a net zero energy future, building one of the leading examples of net zero energy buildings worldwide as their headquarters. Thank you!

This book is the result of the efforts of a number of ILFI staff. Jason F. McLennan, our founder and CEO, worked closely with the Packard Foundation to nurture the idea of this book and continued on to provide overall conceptual direction. Amanda Sturgeon, Executive Director, wrote the introduction and also helped focus the book's intention and content. Brendan Cook, Net Zero Energy Manager, assembled case study content in initial drafts, and Adam Amhrein contributed much of the content of Part III. Emily Doerr and Marisa Hagney supported the effort by compiling baseline technical data and locating images. Jess Chamberlain, a consulting editor, helped refine content and also drafted the Packard Foundation building case study.

A wide array of project team members provided very helpful clarifications to the details of their buildings. Megan Curtis-Murphy of the City of Issaquah, Leah Missik of Built Green, and Will Chin of Puget Sound Energy helped tremendously on getting a second set of billing information for zHome. David Kaneda of Integral Engineering provided helpful clarification regarding the IDeAs Z2 systems. The ever helpful Joe David of Point32 provided significant insight into the development process for the Bullitt Center, and Justin Stenkamp of PAE Engineering and Christopher Meek with the University of Washington Integrated Design Lab had helpful background on the building's occupancy. Dr. Bill Weicking with Hawai'i Preparatory Academy gave new insights and details into the operation of a net zero building five years on. Richard Piacentini helped clarify details of the Phipps CSL atrium. Gerard Lee, then of HED, provided image permissions and information about the West Berkeley Library. Simon Tilley and Trevor Butler provided helpful information and perspectives on the Hockerton Housing Project. Alen Postolka outlined a deep dive explanation of how the Alexandra District Energy system works.

A special shout out goes to Michael D. Berrisford, Ecotone's Editor in Chief. I had the great pleasure of working with Mike on this book, and he is a wonderful combination of enthusiasm, thoughtfulness, courtesy, patience, and firmness. He essentially project managed the assembly of the book, and made sure that the very unusual team drafting process resulted in a cohesive whole. Also of note, are our Creative Director, Erin Gehle, and designer, Johanna Björk, who thoughtfully and skillfully brought elegant design and information together in *The Power of Zero*. Many thanks to Ecotone's Senior Editor, Fred McLennan and to Michael, Erin and Johanna!

Thank you to every owner, design team member, and constructor who had a hand in one of the wonderful buildings in this book. If you have not been involved in one, it is difficult to know how challenging building such a pioneering edifice and vision can be. You are truly climate heroes — thank you for what you did.

Finally, I'd like to thank my wife, Lesli Corthell, for her patience as I've put extracurricular time into the book. I had this great notion of turning our summer vacation into a bit of a writer's retreat, and neglected to fill her in on my vision. On about the fifth day, as I sat writing late into the afternoon, she looked wistfully out at Orcas Island and Lopez Sound and mused about when vacation would begin. I immediately saw the error of my ways. Merci beaucoup mon amour!

BRAD LILJEQUIST

DOMAIN OF
———
KNOWLEDGE

228

LIVING BUILDING CHALLENGE

The International Living Future Institute's Living Building Challenge™ is widely regarded as the built environment's most rigorous building performance standard. The Standard calls for the creation of building projects at all scales to operate as cleanly, beautifully and efficiently as nature's architecture. Living Building Challenge 3.0 is comprised of seven performance areas known as "Petals": Place, Water, Energy, Health & Happiness, Materials, Equity, and Beauty. Petals are subdivided into a total of twenty Imperatives, each of which focuses on a specific sphere of influence. This compilation of Imperatives can be applied to almost every conceivable typology, or project type, be it a building (both renovation of an existing structure or new construction), infrastructure, or landscape.

It is important to note that the ILFI's Standard is not a checklist of best practices—the Imperatives of the Living Building Challenge are performance based and position ideal outcomes as the indicators of success. To earn certification projects are required to meet a series of ambitious performance requirements over a minimum of twelve months of continuous occupancy.

Living Building Challenge projects come in a variety of typologies and consist of both new construction and renovation projects—including historic preservation. Projects include, but are not limited to, single family residences, multi-family residences (market rate and affordable housing), institutional buildings (government, education, research, religious), commercial (offices, retail, hospitality, museums, galleries, botanical gardens), as well as laboratories and medical facilities. These projects can be built in any climate zone anywhere in the world.

Building on the tenets of the Living Building Challenge, the Living Community Challenge provides a broader scale framework for community development. Naturally, strategies to create Living Landscapes, Infrastructure, Renovations, Buildings or Communities will vary widely by occupancy, use, construction type, and location.

LIVING TRANSECTS

Each project participating in the Living Building Challenge, Net Zero Energy Building Certification and the Living Community Challenge must identify its Living Transect, interpreted from the intensity of development surrounding its site. The ILFI has identified six Living Transects, ranging from Natural Habitat Preserve to Urban Core.

Living Transect categories include:

L1. Natural Habitat Preserve (Greenfield sites)

L2. Rural Agriculture Zone

L3. Village or Campus Zone

L4. General Urban Zone

L5. Urban Center Zone

L6. Urban Core Zone

NET ZERO ENERGY BUILDING CERTIFICATION

The building and design industry has characterized net zero energy in many different ways; however, the ILFI subscribes to a simple definition:

One hundred percent of the building's energy needs must be supplied by on-site renewable energy on a net annual basis, without the use of on-site combustion.

The Net Zero Energy Building Certification program uses the structure of the Living Building Challenge 3.0 to document compliance, requiring four of the Imperatives to be achieved: 01, Limits to Growth (not including landscaping requirements); 06, Net Positive Energy (set at 100 percent); 19 Beauty + Spirit; and 20, Inspiration + Education.

Note: The Energy Petal and Living Building Certification requires 105 percent energy production. As with full Living Building Certification and Petal Certification, NZEB certification is based on actual performance rather than modeled outcomes.

GLOSSARY

ASHRAE: The American Society of Heating, Refrigerating, and Air-Conditioning Engineers (ASHRAE) develops performance standards for both its members and others professionally concerned with refrigeration processes and the design and maintenance of indoor environments.

Biomimicry: The Biomimicry Institute defines biomimicry as "an approach to innovation that seeks sustainable solutions to human challenges by emulating nature's time-tested patterns and strategies." Janine Benyus, biologist, author, and co-founder of the Biomimicry Institute, popularized the concept of biomimicry in her 1997 book titled *Biomimicry: Innovation Inspired by Nature*. Today, biomimicry has evolved to a world-wide, bio-inspired sustainable design movement. Nature, in all forms, provides seemingly endless net zero energy examples that designers can learn from and emulate.

Biophilia: Preeminent biologist and author E.O. Wilson coined the term "biophilia" as a word to describe humanity's innate affinity for nature and natural elements such as water, flora, and fauna. Wilson's original biophilia hypothesis (and book by the same name written by Stephen R. Kellert in 1993, *The*

Biophilia Hypothesis, co-edited with E.O. Wilson) illustrated in detail the strong connections between natural and built environments, now referred to as biophilic design.

Building Envelope: The building envelope, also referred to as the building enclosure or outer shell, is comprised of the structural separation between the conditioned and unconditioned environment of a building. Not only does the building envelope function as a resilient barrier for weather and air, it supports mechanical loads and systems, controls thermal transfer and contributes exterior building aesthetics. Climate-appropriate, structurally-sound building envelopes are critical for achieving net zero energy.

Energy Recovery Ventilator (ERV): While HRV systems are ideal for moisture prone indoor environments, energy recovery ventilators are considered more suitable for applications in high humidity and cold climates. ERVs operate in a similar fashion to HRVs; however, they add the additional process of dehumidifying the incoming air.

Energy Use Intensity (EUI): EUI is a building's annual energy use per unit area. EUI is typically measured in thousands of BTU per square foot per year (kBtu/ft2/yr) in the United States, or kWh/m2/yr in most other countries.

As EUI is a valuable metric for comparing the energy performance of buildings across sizes, types, climate zones, and locations, it is fast becoming a vital metric as both an energy performance target and proof.

Heat Recovery Ventilator (HRV): A simple approach to retaining heat and expelling stale air, humidity and pollutants, a heat recovery ventilator is similar to a balanced ventilation system, except it utilizes the heat present in outgoing stale air to warm up the fresh air. A typical HRV unit utilizes two fans, one to expel air from the building, and one to draw in fresh air. The key element of a HRV is its exchange core that acts to transfer heat from the outgoing air to the incoming air. The warmed air is then introduced into the building.

kBtu: Denotes one-thousand British Thermal Units (BTU or Btu). The British Thermal Unit is a traditional unit of energy equal to about 1055 joules, which equals the amount of energy needed to cool or heat one pound of water by one degree Fahrenheit (at a constant pressure of one atmosphere). To determine energy use in a way that enables a comparison of building energy performance, a building's annual energy use intensity is typically calculated in kBtu/sf/year.

kWh: One kilowatt-hour is the volume of electricity equal to one kilowatt flowing for one hour.

Peak Heating and Cooling Loads:
A heating or cooling load is the amount of heat that needs to be added to, or removed from, a space to maintain the desired temperature. The "peak load" is the maximum hourly electrical power demand over the span of a year — so, a building's "peak heating load" is the largest amount of heat that needs to be added to a space in a single hour.

Plug Load: Refers to electricity used by appliances and devices plugged into electrical outlets on a temporary basis by building occupants, typically excluding long-term appliances, such as stoves and refrigerators, which may also use electrical outlets. Also known as "user loads".

R-value: R-value refers to the thermal resistance of a building material, or combined assembly of building materials.

Solar Heat Gain Coefficient (SHGC):
The NFRC describes Solar Heat Gain Coefficient (SHGC) as a measure of how much heat from the sun is blocked by the glazing. SHGC is expressed as a number between 0 and 1; the lower the SHGC, the more effective a product is at blocking solar heat gain. Blocking solar heat gain is particularly important during the summer cooling season in hot southern climates. By contrast, people in northern climates may want solar heat gain during the cold winter months to lessen the cost of heating and to improve thermal comfort.

Thermal Sharing: A strategy by which thermal energy (either hot or cold) is shared between various users through a district system. The energy for the system could be generated specifically to share or as part of a separate, unrelated process. Renewably-based thermal sharing systems generally rely on geothermal, solar thermal, water-source, or sewage-heat recovery.

U-value: The rate of heat loss is indicated in terms of the U-value (also known as the U-factor) of an assembly, typically windows. U-value is the equivalent of 1/the R-value of an assembly. The lower the U-value, the greater a window's resistance to heat flow and the better its insulating properties. The nationally recognized rating method by the National Fenestration Rating Council (NFRC) is for the whole window, including glazing, frame, and spacers. The NFRC states that the U-value measures how effectively a product prevents heat energy from escaping a building. U-value ratings generally fall between 0.15 and 1.20. Center-of-glass U-value is sometimes referenced, and describes the performance of the glazing only, not factoring in the frame assembly.

INTERNATIONAL **LIVING FUTURE** INSTITUTE℠

INTERNATIONAL LIVING FUTURE INSTITUTE

The International Living Future Institute is an environmental NGO committed to catalyzing the transformation toward communities that are socially just, culturally rich, and ecologically restorative. The Institute is premised on the belief that providing a compelling vision for the future is a fundamental requirement for reconciling humanity's relationship with the natural world. The Institute operates the Living Building Challenge, the built environment's most rigorous performance standard, and Declare, an ingredients label for building materials. It houses the Cascadia Green Building Council and Ecotone Publishing.

ECOTONE PUBLISHING

Founded by green building experts in 2004, Ecotone Publishing is dedicated to meeting the growing demand for authoritative and accessible books on sustainable design, materials selection and building techniques in North America and beyond. Located in the Cascadia region, Ecotone is well positioned to play an important part in the green design movement. Ecotone searches out and documents inspiring projects, visionary people, and vital trends that are leading the design industry to transformational change toward a healthier planet.

PHOTOGRAPHY

Arlo K. Abrahamson: p.22

Adam Amrhein: p.18, 209

Farshid Assassi courtesy of BNIM Architects: p.168, 170-173, 226

Jeremy Bitterman: p.78, 80-81, 82, 84, 86-87, 216

Katie Brown: p.184

California High Speed Rail Authority: p.223

Ron Cogswell/Flickr Creative Commons: p.213

Ethan Daniels: p.19

Alexander Denmarsh: p.123, 174, 176, 178, 181-183, 224-225

Joshua Doubek: p.24

Ethan Drinker courtesy of Coldham & Hartman Architects: p.130, 132-134

Todd Eyre: p. 56, 59-59, 61

Dan Farmer courtesy of Bullitt Foundation: p.108, 111, 114-115

Visko Hatfield: p.186 (right)

Thomas Hawk: p.26

Courtesy of Hellmuth+Bicknese Architects: p.124, 127-129

Brocken Inaglory: p.16

iStock: p.194-197, 199

David Kirsch, Flickr Creative Commons: p.222

Nic Lehoux: p.2-3, 102, 105, 107

Brad Liljequist: p.14, 33, 38, 43-45, 47, 49, 201, 203, 206

Mark Luthringer courtesy of Harley Ellis Devereaux: p.4, 166, 192

Gregg Mastorakos Photography, courtesy DPR Construction and SmithGroupJJR: p.88, 90, 91, 92, 94, 95, 192-193

Michael Mathers: p.146, 148-150, 224

Sunshine Mathon: p.50, 52, 54-55

Courtesy of The Miller Hull Partnership: p.8-9, 113

Mathew Millman courtesy of David Baker Architects: p.13, 37, 68, 71, 73-75, 221

Mathew Millman courtesy of Flansburg Architects: p.136, 138-139, 141-143, 145, 192 (inset)

Kevin Miyazaki: p.62, 65, 67

Ed Robinson/OneRedEye: p.218

Brian Rippy: p.116, 119-121

James Santana: p.186 (left), 188

Tara Schmidt: p.20

Brent Smith courtesy of Bullitt Foundation: p.77, 108

Courtesy of Tesla Motors: p.219

U.S. Government: p.21

U.S. Coast Guard: p.23

www.vauban.de, Creative Commons 3.0: p.205

Versar Environmental Management and Construction: p.212

David Wakley courtesy of Harley Ellis Devereaux: p.28-29, 160, 162, 165-167

David Wakley courtesy of Integral Group: p.96, 98-100

Paul g. Weigman: p.214-215

Wikimedia Commons: p.198

Courtesy of WRNS Studio: p.28-29, 152, 154-156, 158-159

DIAGRAMS

Ceres, "Hydraulic Fracturing & Water Stress: Water Demand by the Numbers": p.25

Dar Webb Associates: p.46

Harley Ellis Devereaux: p.163

ILFI: p.10, 11, 18, 31, 35 (right), 48, 112, 180, 189, 190-191, 207, 208-211, 220

The Miller Hull Partnership: p.34-35

PAE Engineering: p.30

City of Richmond: p.200